The Instruction

AINSLIE MACLEOD

THE
INSTRUCTION

Living the Life Your Soul Intended

SOUNDS TRUE
awakening wisdom

Sounds True, Inc.
Boulder, CO 80306

© 2007 Ainslie MacLeod

SOUNDS TRUE is a trademark of Sounds True, Inc.

All rights reserved. Published 2007.
Printed in Canada

Jacket design © 2007 MacLeod Nine Inc.
Book design by Chad Morgan

ISBN 978-1-59179-605-3

Library of Congress Cataloging-in-Publication Data

MacLeod, Ainslie, 1954–

 The instruction : living the life your soul intended / Ainslie MacLeod.

  p. cm.

 ISBN 978-1-59179-605-3 (hardcover)

 1. Guides (Spiritualism) 2. Soul. I. Title.

BF1275.G85M33 2007

133.9—dc22

                              2007018217

To Lisa, Kyra, and Lucas, with all my love

CONTENTS

ACKNOWLEDGMENTS

When I began asking my clients if they'd like to be in my book, the one phrase I kept hearing was, "I'd be honored." Well, I can truly say that the feeling is mutual. I feel privileged to be part of your journeys, and I thank you for allowing me to share your often very personal and moving stories.

I want to give special thanks to my soulmate, Lisa, and my family and friends for all their love and support.

I'd like to thank my agent, Eric Myers, for his expert guidance, and my editor, Kelly Notaras, for her enthusiasm and invaluable advice. I give my thanks, also, to everyone at Sounds True for all their tremendous efforts.

I'm indebted to the many psychics I've had the good fortune to meet over the years, particularly Bettina Luxon and David Walton.

And to my spirit guides: without you this book would not have been possible. I thank you from the depths of my soul for your wisdom, encouragement, and patience.

INTRODUCTION
The Reluctant Psychic

like a ship without a compass, most of us sail blindly through life with no real idea of where we're going.

Then, every so often, we run aground and assume we've reached our destination.

We all search for happiness. Yet few goals are quite as elusive. Often we think we've found it, only to lose it again, or to realize we never really had it in the first place. For some of us, happiness keeps turning to disappointment. For others, happiness is always around the next corner.

We'll spend years getting an education and training for the career we've always dreamed of, then end up stuck in a job we hate. We'll search the world for true love, only to get tangled up in a five-year relationship that shouldn't have lasted five minutes.

The problem is that most of us don't know what it is we actually want. We end up sailing from one place to the next, hoping to find who or what we're looking for through luck rather than design.

The Instruction offers an alternative to this hit-or-miss approach. It explains how to create a happier and more purposeful life by finding out who you are and why you're here.

But how?

Like everyone else on the planet, you have a soul. And what your soul wants is for you to follow the life plan it created before you were born. Your life plan is the map your soul uses to help you navigate the Physical Plane: the three-dimensional world your body and conscious mind inhabit.

Your life plan has clearly defined elements, yet it allows for total free will. It includes a complete personality, a set of goals, challenges to be overcome, people to meet, fears to be faced, and lessons to be learned.

To discover who you are and why you're here, all you have to do is look at your life plan—which is precisely what this book will show you how to do. It will walk you through the ten elements of your life plan, and reveal the secrets of living the life your soul intended.

What's the importance of living the life your soul intended? The answer is that by understanding your soul's purpose, you'll no longer sail aimlessly through life. Instead of being that ship without a compass, you'll set course knowing your current location, your destination, and what you're going to do when you get there.

To discover what your soul wants, I'm going to take you on a journey to the Soul World, a place where the answers to all of life's mysteries can be found. As we step through each of twelve doors, I'll reveal the Instruction, a unique system given to me by elevated spirit guides. Its purpose is to help you better understand yourself and enhance your experience of life on earth.

By the time the journey is complete, you'll have discovered who you are and why you're here; how to overcome many of life's challenges; and how to use what you've learned to live the life your soul intended.

But first, a little about who *I* am and why *I'm* here.

Lost at Sea

In the mid-1990s, I arrived in California amid a cloud of emotional pain and confusion. Behind me was a two-decade-long trail of drama, heartache, and disappointment. Ahead of me I could see nothing but more of the same.

Then I had an epiphany: an incident that literally changed my life.

Ten years earlier, I'd been a cartoon illustrator living and working in central London. On a trip to Brighton on England's south coast, I met a gifted psychic named David Walton. In a dimly lit shop basement, I sat opposite him as he relayed messages from spirit guides on the other side. Everything he said struck me as being astonishingly accurate. That is, until he predicted something so unlikely I couldn't imagine it would ever happen.

He said, "You're going to end up in California."

When I told him the idea didn't particularly appeal to me, he leaned forward, shook his head gravely, and added, "There is nothing you can do about it. Nothing."

A decade later, I found myself in a tiny studio, nestled in an alleyway under the imposing shadow of San Francisco's landmark Fairmont Hotel. The room was eerily silent—so much so that I could hear my heart beating.

I was stressed out to the point that I could barely think straight. I slumped down on the sofa and wondered what to do next. It had been years since I'd meditated, but it seemed as good a time as any to start again. I closed my eyes and took a couple of deep breaths.

That was when I heard David Walton's words as clearly as when he'd first said them: "You're going to end up in California. There is nothing you can do about it. Nothing."

I shot to my feet, as a wave of adrenaline shocked me out my inertia. I looked around, half imagining I wasn't alone. After a minute or so, I calmed down enough to think more rationally. That was when I realized I was living a psychic's prediction of my life.

. . .

Growing up in Aberdeen, Scotland, I had many psychic experiences, though I never saw them as such. I read newspaper articles convinced I'd seen them a week before, and I often knew what would be playing on the radio alarm clock before it switched itself on.

My first impressions of people were usually right, though I always had the tendency to override my intuition and see the best in everybody. ("You're too good for this world," my favorite aunt would say.) And I often knew what people were going to say before they said it. I had to learn to bite my tongue and wait until someone had actually posed a question before I answered it.

When I was sixteen, a man in a thirties-style hat and coat approached me at a table in the reference library and, despite the no-smoking sign, asked for a light. He kept looking away furtively as if he were being followed, so I couldn't really see his face. I searched my pockets for matches, and when I looked up, he'd completely vanished.

When I asked the lady sitting beside me if she'd seen where he'd gone, she didn't know what I was talking about. It would be years before I learned that I'd seen a ghost, one who'd approached me because he knew I'd be able to see him.

Despite all of this, I never thought I was psychic. I didn't particularly enjoy any of these experiences; they simply left me confused and unsettled. In fact, because I could see so many things before they occurred, I used to wonder if I somehow made them happen. ("If I hadn't spent the last hour thinking about the car getting a flat tire, it might never have happened.")

When it came to making wise choices, my lack of understanding and natural tendency to ignore my intuition made me quite inept. Actually, it was worse than that. My intuition might tell me one thing, but I'd do the exact opposite.

Around the time I left home to become an art student, I met the girl who would become my first wife. What she saw in me I don't know. She was pretty, well-groomed, and highly intelligent. I was spotty and kind of frayed around the edges; my hair was down to my waist, and I smelled of Winsor and Newton oil paints. Still, opposites attract, as they say.

We married (against my better judgment) and, almost immediately, the relationship took a nosedive. To my utter incomprehension, her affection for me was replaced with hostility, and over the next three years I suffered a constant barrage of put-downs, criticism, ridicule, and sexual humiliation.

By the time we split up, I was a bag of nerves, and my self-confidence was nowhere to be found.

Like many sensitive people, I'd grown up hearing I was "too sensitive." By this time, I was in full agreement. I blamed my "flaw" for the state I was in. To ensure I'd never be hurt like that again, I decided to reinvent myself by adopting a protective alter ego. Out went the gentle idealist, and in came a tough-talking, cynical new me.

I surrounded myself with noise and drama to block out my feelings. I played in rock bands and partied every night. I bought a convertible sports car and took to wearing a black leather jacket to look more macho.

I hoped to insulate myself from my emotions by denying who I was. In doing so, I severed contact with the spirit world and that part of me that was psychic.

From then on, I was on my own. Like a leather-clad Mr. Magoo, I blundered through the next couple of decades, taking every wrong turn and making every possible bad decision.

I began dating lots of women, hoping to find Miss Right. There was a schizophrenic, a junkie, plenty of alcoholics, a dominatrix, two who tried to kill themselves, and one who tried to kill me.

People warned me about my self-destructive behavior, but I wouldn't listen. To paraphrase an old blues song, I'd been down so long it all looked like up to me.

Though I never met Miss Right, I started bumping into psychics wherever I went. On one occasion, a woman sidled up to me in a crowded London pub, introduced herself as a fellow psychic, and told me I should be doing it professionally. Me? A professional psychic? I thought she was mad.

Yet, despite my cynicism, I found psychics fascinating. Around that time, I started making regular visits to a gifted clairvoyant named Bettina Luxon. Every time I sat down at the kitchen table in her cramped North London flat, she'd tell me I was psychic. I used to joke, "If I was psychic I wouldn't be here."

Yet Bettina was insistent. With her encouragement, I began practicing such things as separating a pack of cards into piles of red and black, face down. The results were quite encouraging. I even managed to successfully read a couple of people.

Then, before I could develop my skills any further, my life spiraled out of control once again.

Despite warnings from David Walton and Bettina, I got involved with a sociopath. (When they told me she had no conscience and could never be trusted, I heroically jumped to her defense.) On one of our first dates, she got blind drunk and kicked me in the balls so hard I nearly passed out. Most people would have taken that as a warning sign. Not me. Thanks to my dismally low self-confidence and abusive past, I didn't believe I deserved much better.

If I'd listened to my intuition, I would never have let her within fifty feet of me. As it was, I didn't trust my judgment—or that of the psychics. And once again, any intuitive ability I might have had vanished as my life became one long round of verbal abuse and physical threats.

I financed her business, and after four insane years she brought the whole thing crashing down. (She'd tried to start it up elsewhere under a similar name to write off the debt I was owed.) I lost the lot: the business, my savings, my home, and my possessions.

So, when I met the New Yorker who was to become my second wife, I had nothing to keep me in London. I emigrated to the States like generations of Scots before me.

For the first time in my life, I felt I'd found true happiness. She was affectionate, supportive, and highly entertaining. I used to joke that she was the person for whom the word "eccentric" was created. Unfortunately she was also severely alcoholic.

On our wedding day, literally minutes after we tied the knot, my new bride got into a scrap with a taxi driver and tried to drag the poor guy out of his cab. It was another warning sign, but I was blinded by love, and quickly convinced myself that everything was going to be just fine.

It wasn't, of course. Our five years together began with high hopes, but as time went on the bad times began to outweigh the good. Moments of tenderness and intimacy were overshadowed by her alcohol-fueled rages and blackouts. My ability to use my sixth sense had resurfaced briefly, but soon, overstimulated by noise and chaos, it disappeared beneath the surface once again.

Finally, things deteriorated to the point that I called Bettina in London. Before I could even tell her what was going on, she said, "Get out now—before you get hurt." This time I didn't ignore her.

And a week later I was in California.

Who Died and Made Me an Expert?

The epiphany that took place on my first night in San Francisco inspired me to begin exploring the world beyond. I wanted to know how it was that psychics do what they do. How can anyone tell the future? Where do they get their information?

I took a recommended reading list I'd been given by a psychic I'd met in Atlanta and loaded up on books I hoped would help answer my questions. Some of them were full of nothing but vacuous blather; others were total eye-openers. I read a book a day for several months.

During that period I'd been working hard, illustrating Chester Cheetah for Frito-Lay from my temporary office in the corner of Kinko's copy shop on Van Ness Avenue. After the job was delivered, I decided to take a break. I packed a bag and headed for Hawaii.

The psychics had always told me that my deceased Uncle John was one of my spirit guides. Kathleen Loughery, a trance channeler I met on the island of Kauai, was no different. Toward the end of my session with her, she said, "Your uncle is here, and he's ready to start working with you."

I left Kathleen and walked out into the glaring sunshine in what I recognized to be a slightly altered state. I drove (cautiously) to Borders bookstore and, as I stood facing a bookshelf, suddenly saw a face to my right.

I froze in amazement. It was my Uncle John, looking just like he had twenty years before. The image was dimensional and sharp, though it only lasted a second or two at the most. At the same time I got a message: "Let's get started."

So I did.

I moved into the tranquility of a houseboat in Sausalito, just north of the Golden Gate Bridge, where I gradually regained my confidence and, along with it, my old self.

I spent the next two years learning to communicate with what John described as the Soul World. John is currently on the Astral Plane, where those who are between lives prepare for their next incarnation. He introduced me to my elevated spirit guides on the Causal Plane, the next level beyond. This is where those who have completed all their lives on the Physical Plane eventually go to become guides and teachers.

The Three Planes

Throughout this book, I'll be discussing three planes of existence. They are:

The Physical Plane
The first and most solid plane is the three-dimensional world we inhabit here on earth.

The Astral Plane
The Astral Plane is the nearest non-physical world to this. It's where we go when we die, and is the home to Astral guides.

The Causal Plane
When we've completed all our incarnations on the Physical Plane, we move beyond the Astral to the Causal Plane, where we eventually become elevated spirit guides.

Our guides on the Causal Plane have access to everything in our soul's life plan. They know all about us: our fears and hopes, our successes and disappointments, and, above all, what we're here to achieve.

And though I found accessing the Causal Plane a good deal harder than the Astral Plane, the rewards were much greater. Not only could I understand what other people were all about, I got to see where I'd gone wrong in my own life.

The source of all my problems, I found out, was my inability to accept myself and my purpose. Instead of choosing partners, for example, who appreciated my gentler qualities, I'd always gone for those who I hoped would help me be something I wasn't. No wonder things had a habit of not working out.

As I gradually learned to be myself again, my life was transformed. I began to make wiser choices, simply because I knew myself and what was in my best interest. And as I explored my life plan, one of the most significant things I discovered was that I really was being guided to become a professional psychic.

But, why me? Why was I chosen to do this work? The answer is that, when it comes to drifting off course, I've truly been there and done that. In my Causal guides' views, my own personal experience, combined with my natural gift, made me well qualified to help others get their lives on track.

Yet it was in this particular area that self-acceptance issues continued to surface. When, at long last, I felt ready to embrace my destiny, I found one thing still holding me back: my utter embarrassment at actually being a psychic!

I'd finally overcome my resistance, and accepted my calling, but now I cringed every time I saw my name in print: "Ainslie MacLeod, Psychic Guide." *Why on earth,* I'd wonder, *couldn't I have been "Jim Smith, Plumber"?*

So, if you think talking to invisible entities in the Soul World is weird, join the club. I still find it quite bizarre that I've ended up doing this. Yet I have to admit I feel profoundly privileged to have this fantastic opportunity. My job is endlessly fascinating, and my learning curve is on a permanent 45-degree trajectory.

The skeptic in me remembers how I used to read a book like this and wonder, *Who died and made this guy an expert?* The answer, in my case, is . . . my spirit guides. I'm simply the messenger. I'm not a psychologist, a therapist, a guru, or anything other than just a psychic and a serious investigator of the soul.

This book doesn't describe any kind of philosophy or religion. It's nothing more than my interpretation of information given to me by my Causal spirit guides, illustrated by examples from sessions with my clients.

But why, you might ask, should you believe what my spirit guides have to say? The answer is validation. Let me give you an example.

A few years ago, a young woman came to see me with general life questions. Nothing much my guides said could be immediately verified. Then, to her surprise, they told her she was pregnant. She just smiled and shook her head. Less than a week later, however, she found out they were right.

The reason they told her this was to help her accept all the other information they'd given her. But, of course, not everyone can get such immediate validation.

When I talk about there being billions of souls throughout the universe, or that humans on Earth only began to have souls fifty-five thousand years ago, I can't prove any of that. I'm simply quoting my spirit guides.

Are they asking you to suspend disbelief and simply accept what they tell you? Certainly not. They want you to question everything and continually ask yourself if the information rings true. By doing that, validation will come from you, using your own intuition.

When I agreed to devote the rest of my life to being a psychic and exploring the soul, I was offered, in return, a key to the Soul

World. It has allowed me to access everything from the reason we have an appendix to why we go to war. But most of all, it's helped me understand what each of us is doing here.

So if, like me, you have a thirst for knowledge and a hunger to learn the purpose of your existence, allow me to be your guide on an amazing voyage of discovery.

Together we'll investigate the mystery of who you are and why you're here, and uncover the secret of living the life your soul intended.

The Instruction

The Instruction is designed to give those who are open to it
an understanding of how the Spiritual Universe works,
and to help those on the Physical Plane
become more connected to their soul's purpose.
—THE AUTHOR'S CAUSAL SPIRIT GUIDES

One evening, my spirit guides ended a session by telling me to take a five-day break. During that period I couldn't access them at all.

Five days later they were back, and this time they spoke British English, rather than American English. They told me about a system they called the Instruction, and that I was to become its teacher.

I channeled the outline of the system over a three-week period, and its many subtleties were explained to me during months of subsequent sessions with my spirit guides.

When describing the elements that make up *The Instruction*, I've tried, as much as possible, to "show rather than tell." For that reason, I've used real-life examples from sessions with clients throughout, changing only the names and some identifying details for reasons of privacy.

The Instruction offers complex information expressed in a simple way. Making sense of it doesn't require a degree in metaphysics, yet there are a number of terms that are used frequently in the Instruction that you should know about:

The Illusion

The Illusion is the barrier between the Physical Plane and the Soul World. It prevents enlightenment, or the recognition that all humanity is connected. Everyone is vulnerable to becoming caught up in it.

The Illusion breaks down when exposed to introspection, which is why certain souls are more able to overcome its influence than others.

The Instruction is a way for any person to break through the Illusion and achieve enlightenment. The secret is to be willing to try.

Advantages and Risks

Each element of the Instruction has an advantage and a risk. The advantage is what can be achieved by following your soul's guidance.

Risks are essentially the absence of the soul's influence. Advantages can be used to turn around a long-standing risk and help an individual to live the life his or her soul intended.

The Soul World

Throughout this book, you'll come across the term "Soul World," which is used by my spirit guides to describe that part of the spiritual universe that contains both your soul and your spirit guides.

Politics and the Soul

It's impossible to discuss the soul without exploring political and social attitudes. As you'll discover, nothing shapes your beliefs like the influence of your soul.

An inescapable fact is that younger souls tend to be more conservative, while older souls are usually more progressive.

I want to make it clear that when I discuss politics and the soul, I have no agenda. In presenting my understanding of the way the soul affects us, I've tried to be as even-handed as I possibly can be.

Enlightenment

The ultimate purpose of the Instruction is enlightenment.

And what exactly is enlightenment? Well, according to my spirit guides, if you can manifest your soul's age and type, embrace the goals and lessons your soul chose for you in this lifetime, overcome the obstacles and distractions in your way, and act out of love rather than fear, you've got it.

Enlightenment, to put it simply, comes from living the life your soul intended. The Instruction is the key.

A Simple Meditation Technique

The great philosopher Confucius said, "I hear and I forget. I see and I remember. I do and I understand." This is the reason that the Instruction requires some level of involvement on your part.

As you travel through each of the doors in this book, you'll be encouraged to answer questions and undertake a number of simple exercises. They'll help you to assimilate the knowledge you receive in a deeper way than simply reading about it. These exercises require you to meditate and call in your spirit guides.

A student of the Dalai Lama once asked him, "What is the best way to meditate?"

"Whatever works for you," he replied.

For the purposes of the Instruction, however, it's better to avoid using a mantra, background music, or a guided meditation. The aim is to still your mind so your spirit guides can work with you.

The following is a simple method my spirit guides suggest. They call it the Open Heart meditation, where you open up to your spirit guides to receive their assistance.

1. Sit upright in a comfortable chair, your hands cupped in your lap. Close your eyes and take a few deep breaths. Bring in your spirit guides using the following words: "I call upon my spirit guides, acting in my highest interest, to join me in my meditation."
2. Ask your spirit guides to give you tranquility and clarity.
3. Once you sense their presence (a feeling of tranquility and clarity), ask your spirit guides to answer your specific question. For example, "Please help me identify my soul type."
4. Then ask your spirit guides to help you complete the exercise that follows.
5. When you've finished. Thank your spirit guides, and tell them, "Session over." (The reason for doing this is so that you don't go back into the physical world in an altered state.)

Allow me to address some frequently asked questions on the subject. First, your spirit guides will communicate by giving you clarity, not by using words. If you don't achieve some degree of clarity in twenty minutes (and it shouldn't take anything like that long if you're already relaxed), stop and try again later.

How do you know if the meditation is working? You should sense the company of your spirit guides. It'll be subtle, but along with clarity and tranquility, you'll gradually become aware that you're not totally alone.

Every single person, no matter who he or she is, has spirit guides who want to work with them. You're no exception. Your spirit guides are actively interested in helping you. You only have to ask. Consider them as friends who care deeply about you.

It's best not to call in your guides for these exercises if you're in a crowded place like a train, or at work. You'll get the best results when you're alone.

And here's one last piece of advice from my own spirit guides: "Use intuition, not intellect, in all cases." What they mean is that the kind of clarity you get from them is sensed on a gut level, rather than resulting from lengthy analysis.

The first destination on our journey through the Soul World, takes us to a place where you can attain true self-understanding. By uncovering your life's purpose, you'll achieve a sense of direction that will lead you confidently toward the future your soul has planned for you.

PART 1: DIRECTION

1: THE DOOR TO CONSCIOUSNESS
Investigating the Soul's Existence

*Souls can be found throughout the universe in numbers that are
so large they cannot be comprehended. Regardless of their location,
all souls have the same purpose: to evolve.*

—THE AUTHOR'S CAUSAL GUIDES

The universe is bigger than any of us can possibly imagine. And though it might seem empty and remote, the reality is very different.

The cosmos is packed with excitement. And it's not just colliding galaxies, bubbling nebulas, collapsing suns, and ferocious black holes. Throughout the universe there is life: living species and great civilizations, chaos and crisis, noise and clutter, struggles and drama in abundance.

The Door to Consciousness leads to the awareness that the universe is a place of infinite possibilities, and that what we see here on the Physical Plane is just a very small part of it.

Scientists currently estimate there to be seventy thousand million million million stars out there, and the actual number might be much greater. That's at least ten stars for every grain of sand on all the beaches and deserts on our entire planet. (Think about it the next time you're on the beach.)

Some Perspective

If you left planet Earth in a spaceship traveling at the speed of light, you'd reach the moon in a couple of seconds. About eight minutes later you'd zip past the sun, ninety-three million miles away. If you started out after breakfast, you'd easily make it to Pluto, way out there at the edge of our solar system, in time for dinner.

How much longer do you think it would take to cross our galaxy, the Milky Way? Another few hours? A day or two? A week? A month? Several years? No, to cross the Milky Way would take you a good one-hundred thousand years. And remember, that's at the speed of light.

If, however, you wanted to see what's at the very edge of the known universe, you'd still be traveling billions of years later.

The universe is vast. Once you start to get a grasp of just how big it is, the idea that there are other species sharing it with us isn't that hard to accept.

The single reason that the universe is so full of living creatures is that life is simply not that hard to create.

Back in the 1950s, Stanley Miller, a professor of chemistry and biochemistry working in a lab at the University of Chicago, conducted an experiment designed to recreate the circumstances that gave rise to life on our planet.

He added an electrical spark to a mixture of hydrogen, methane, ammonia, and water vapor and came up with the amino acids that are found in the proteins that create living matter.

As a result of his experiments, Professor Miller became confident that life could be found in abundance throughout the universe. Some people have questioned Miller's assumptions about the chemical makeup of Earth's early atmosphere. Nevertheless, it's clear that, given the right circumstances, life can emerge from a few simple elements.

Wherever life takes hold, it multiplies. Our little planet is proof of that. It's home to an enormous variety of species, of which 2.1 million have been classified. The actual number could be as large as one hundred million. Species are dying out before we've even had the chance to discover them.

Is it really surprising then, given the scale of the universe and the fact that life flourishes when it gets the opportunity, that there would be billions of species with souls out there?

In our galaxy alone, there are between twenty and thirty million species with souls: conscious, rational beings, aware of their own individuality.

So, where do they all come from?

The soul is part of a consciousness that fills every part of the universe. It permeates the Physical Plane by the process in which species become ensouled.
—THE AUTHOR'S CAUSAL GUIDES

The soul's purpose is to evolve. And the only way to do that is to experience life on the Physical Plane. It's not enough to simply observe our world and hope to know what it's like to be here. To really find out what being human is all about, a soul has to leave the Universal Consciousness and become part of a physical body.

Once it does this, the game begins. The soul will then be here for a complete chain of lives, during which it will be exposed to everything the Physical Plane can throw at it.

Although it will briefly visit the Astral Plane between incarnations, the soul won't rejoin the Universal Consciousness until all its lives here are completed.

Personal Evidence of the Soul's Existence

So, how do we know the soul even exists? For some people, there is simply no question. David is just one of several of my clients who has had firsthand experience that has left him with no doubts whatsoever.

I know you must have heard this kind of story before. In this medically advanced world of ours, more people than ever are being brought back to life after dying. In fact, near death experiences are getting to be so common, you might even know someone who had one.

But the reason I include David's account of his near death experience is to illustrate how such an event can shape the entire course of an individual's life.

David was eleven years old when he became the first kid in his Long Island neighborhood to have a ten-speed bike. On a Monday afternoon in 1967, he left home on his bike to go to the store. The time was 3:05. He remembers nothing that happened after that.

An hour later, at exactly 4:05, David was hit by a car. The driver was so drunk she didn't realize she'd hit him, or that she'd dragged him forty feet.

When the police turned up, David had no pulse and his breathing had stopped. They pulled a sheet over his face and had his body taken to the hospital.

As they broke the bad news to his mother, David's hand suddenly fell from the stretcher beside them. Within seconds, doctors and nurses leaped into action and began trying to resuscitate him.

Meanwhile, David was undergoing a classic near death experience, or NDE.

Immediately after the accident, David found himself "suspended in black," experiencing a profound sense of peace. He sensed he was moving, but couldn't see anything. After a while, he began traveling toward a bright white light. He could sense a presence behind it.

As he looked into the light, he heard himself say, "I'm not ready yet." He gradually turned until the light was behind him, and started moving away from it. He felt the light slowly fade away until he was suspended in black once more.

He peered down and saw himself lying in a hospital bed, with his mother and his best friend's mother standing facing him. He gradually floated back into his body, opened his eyes, and asked, "What am I doing here?"

When David told me the story, he stopped at this point to stress that the whole experience hadn't been in the least scary, and even when he came back to his physical body, he still had the over-whelming sensation of tranquility.

Many people who have experienced NDEs have talked about returning with a clear understanding of what their life is about. As an eleven-year-old, David was no exception. "I knew I had a purpose—a job to do," he told me. "I wanted to help people, and I decided then to become a doctor. And I also wanted to fly. That wasn't anything to do with the NDE. I'd been obsessed with flying since I was five."

He joined the Navy, became a fighter pilot, and graduated as a doctor from the Uniformed Services University of the Health Sciences. He then fulfilled another ambition by becoming a flight surgeon.

Since his NDE, David has consistently followed his soul's direction to help others. Recently, as an obstetrican, he's begun using cutting-edge craniosacral therapy in the delivery room, with astonishing results.

"I've never been conventional," he said. "I've always felt compelled to do what I was compelled to do. What the NDE did for me was to make me sure that what I'm doing is what I'm supposed to be doing."

In many ways, David was fortunate. Not only did his NDE give him a clear insight into the life his soul had planned for him, but it allowed him to experience what it's like to survive death—to be conscious, yet separate from his body.

But what about those of us who haven't been to the other side and back? How can we discover our soul's purpose? How can we be certain that such a thing as a soul even exists?

Searching for the Soul

A March 11, 1907 *New York Times* article describes a doctor named MacDougall, who claimed to have weighed the soul. He placed his dying patients on a bed, which sat on a giant set of scales. At the moment of death, Dr. MacDougall found his patients suddenly lost as much as an ounce.

I'm no scientist, but I can tell you with certainty that the soul weighs nothing. It exists as energy. A cup of soul would weigh as much as a cup of electricity, which is nothing—and also beside the point. Proof of the soul's existence is not going to come from weighing the dead and dying.

On the other hand, plenty of evidence for there being a soul comes from those who have died and come back.

The relative ease with which some children can communicate with the spirit world extends to their own souls. Often children can recall a past life with such accuracy that investigators can validate it—especially when the location is close to where they currently live.

One such investigator, Dr. Ian Stevenson, author of *Twenty Cases Suggestive of Reincarnation,* has documented thousands of claims of past-life memories. He spent years traveling around India investigating, in a thoroughly scientific manner, children who remembered people and locations from previous lives.

Stevenson interviewed many children who claimed to belong elsewhere, or who had difficulty accepting their humble circumstances after a lifetime of greater affluence. He witnessed children being reunited with their previous families, often identifying individuals by their nicknames, or being able to describe changes made to the family home since their death.

A fellow academic is quoted as saying once said of Dr. Stevenson, "Either he is making a colossal mistake, or he will be known as the Galileo of the twentieth century."

He may be right, but let's look, for a moment, at the Galileo of the seventeenth century.

Long before Galileo, humans knew of the existence of most of the planets in our solar system. On a clear night, they could see Mars, Mercury, Venus, Jupiter, and Saturn. That still left three more planets to be discovered (or perhaps two, now that Pluto has been downgraded). But with no way to get a closer view, that was the accepted view of the universe for thousands of years.

Galileo became the first astronomer to view the night sky with a telescope, radically altering our understanding of the universe.

As for the soul, it can't be seen at all. No new and improved optical device is going to suddenly bring it into view. Without weight, mass, or density, it can't be seen, touched, or measured.

In fact, it could be argued that the soul doesn't exist at all.

And neither does the planet Neptune.

Except, of course, that it does. But that wasn't always the case. It was only discovered in the nineteenth century. Not, initially, because astronomers actually saw it, but because they noticed irregularities in the orbit of Uranus.

In the same way that fluctuations in the orbit of Uranus pointed to the existence of Neptune, the soul's existence can be demonstrated not by examining it directly, but by observing its invisible influence on the part of us that we can see: our beliefs and behavior.

Like Neptune, and all the other planets, the soul has always been there. Humans just haven't formally discovered it yet.

But what exactly is the soul? And what does it do for us?

Its most significant effect is to make us creatures of almost unlimited reason. Rats may learn to press a certain button for food, and chimps may be able to use a stick to catch termites, but we've learned to build computer chips, create complex societies, and explore this and other planets.

None of this would have happened without a soul to keep pushing us forward. Its purpose is to evolve, and whether we like it or not, that's our purpose too.

Like an iceberg, the biggest part of you—your soul—is hidden beneath the surface. It exerts its influence silently, yet it affects every single thing you do. It gives you your individuality, your personality, and your ability for abstract thought.

It's the age and type of the soul, and the degree to which we connect with it, that gives us all such radically differing views of the world. It's the reason one person will risk imprisonment to protest a war, while another will eagerly volunteer for combat.

It's what made Mother Teresa devote her life to helping the poor, while Donald Trump devotes his to making money. It's why one person will hold a candlelight vigil outside death row to protest an execution, while a DJ at a radio station celebrates the event by playing "Another One Bites the Dust."

Your soul influences where you live, your choice of friends and partners, what job you do, how you vote, who or what you worship, and where you stand on issues like stem cell research and abortion. In other words, everything.

Which is why, if you're ever going to figure out your purpose in life, it's essential to understand who you are on a soul level.

In the next chapter, we'll investigate the first of the ten elements that make up the Instruction, and discover how multiple lifetimes of hardship, joy, love, death, and countless other experiences affect the way you see the world.

2: THE DOOR TO PERCEPTION
Soul Ages: The Source of Your Beliefs

Beliefs are a result of the soul's influence, and are what gives
people their perspective on the world. No two people share exactly
the same beliefs. Each individual believes the world is as they see it,
yet they understand just a small part of it.

—THE AUTHOR'S CAUSAL GUIDES

The Door to Perception opens to reveal the seemingly perplexing world of beliefs.

Before I discovered the source of our beliefs, I used to scratch my head and wonder why two people of similar intelligence and education could end up being poles apart politically and socially.

What made one person join the NRA and another the Brady Campaign to Prevent Gun Violence?

Why would two people see the world so differently that one would become a right-wing Republican, and the other a liberal Democrat?

And why do you always seem to get a complete package? Why is it that if someone holds fundamentalist religious views, you can predict where they stand on abortion, gay marriage, the death penalty, and the right to bear arms?

And speaking of religion, why are there six major faiths and not just one?

When I discovered the answer, the wide spectrum of beliefs that appears to be unique to our species suddenly made complete sense.

Let's take a look at some examples of this diversity.

"The death penalty is both cruel and unnecessary. The dignity of human life must never be taken away, even in the case of someone who has done great evil."

—POPE JOHN PAUL II

"The death penalty is our society's recognition of the sanctity of human life."

—SENATOR ORRIN HATCH OF UTAH

"Marijuana is one of the safest therapeutically active substances known to man."

—JUDGE FRANCIS YOUNG OF THE DRUG ENFORCEMENT AGENCY

"All casual drug users should be taken out and shot."

— DARYL GATES, FORMER LOS ANGELES POLICE CHIEF

"What greater pain could mortals have than this: to see their children dead before their eyes?"

—EURIPIDES, THE PHILOSOPHER

"Well, they're just Communists. They deserve to die."

—JESSE HELMS, FORMER U.S. SENATOR (ON THE MURDER OF A GROUP OF NICARAGUAN CHILDREN, DOCTORS, AND NURSES)

"Each one of them is Jesus in a distressing disguise."

—MOTHER TERESA (ON PEOPLE WITH AIDS)

"AIDS is the wrath of a just God against homosexuals."

—REVEREND JERRY FALWELL

There we have it: life is sacred—and we have to kill people to uphold that ideal.

Marijuana is beneficial—and its users should be taken out and shot.

There is nothing worse than the sight of a dead child—unless its beliefs are contrary to your own.

And AIDS sufferers are on a par with Jesus—yet deserve to die.

It probably goes without saying that, when it comes to our beliefs, we humans are the most diverse species on the planet.

Our beliefs both unite us and divide us. They're at the root of all our conflicts, whether they're religious, political, or ideological, and yet they'll bring us together in places of worship and political and social organizations.

The conviction that our way is the only way can lead us to take extreme measures against those who don't see the world the way we do. Centuries ago, the Crusaders slaughtered their way through the Middle East, convinced of the righteousness of their cause. And in 1568, the entire population of the Netherlands was condemned to death by the Pope in an attempt to stamp out Calvinism.

We'll even put our beliefs before our own lives. Buddhist monks burned themselves alive to protest the Vietnam War, and in the Middle East, suicide bombers kill themselves along with others for the sake of their cause.

But where do our beliefs come from? Is it the influence of our parents and how we're brought up? If that were the case, you'd expect siblings to agree on everything. And if you have a brother or a sister, you'll know how unlikely that is.

It can't be the result of education. College graduates disagree with each other all the time.

And it's not just a question of intelligence, either. If it were, all people with an IQ of 104 would see eye to eye on everything.

Quite simply, your beliefs are a reflection of how old you are on a soul level, and to what degree you're caught up in the Illusion, the barrier between this plane and the next.

In the same way that a five-year-old sees the world very differently from a senior citizen, a young soul has an outlook on life quite unlike that of an old soul.

But how does one soul get to be older than the next?

The answer is reincarnation. The key to our evolution is the fact that we can come back to this plane time and time again to learn what it is to be human.

Your soul wants a master's degree—not an evening class. If it only had one lifetime here, it wouldn't really learn very much. Thanks to reincarnation, however, each of us will get a well-rounded education over many, many lifetimes.

Why You See the World the Way You Do

Several thousand years and many lifetimes ago, you came into the world as a Level 1 soul. And by the time you leave, at the end of Level 10, you might have something like 120 to 150 lives behind you.

Your soul's evolutionary path takes the soul from a state of fear to one of love, from acting out of self-interest to altruism. On its journey, its understanding of the world is in a state of constant flux.

One lifetime might, for example, teach your soul what it's like to be unfairly imprisoned. From then on, it will have a greater sense of injustice. Another life might be spent as a government official, learning about power and authority. In this way, every lifetime builds upon the last, to create multiple layers of awareness.

A Word about Soul Ages

In this world where youth is worshipped, many people want to be
younger than they are. Yet when it comes to the soul, suddenly everyone wants to be old. So let me state as clearly as possible:

- Your soul age is what it is.
- An old soul is no better or worse than a young soul.
- If you're an old soul now, you were once a young soul and saw the
  world from a young soul's perspective.

The soul ages are broken down into two halves or chains: young and
old. A chain contains five levels, each of which may take as few as
five or as many as twenty lifetimes to complete, depending on the
rate at which objectives are achieved. Like the links in a piece of
jewelry, each level is separate, yet connected to the whole.

Once the major lesson of each level is absorbed, it will become
a permanent part of the soul's experience. Level 2, for example, is
all about learning to cooperate with others. From that point on, an
understanding of the importance of cooperation will be with the
soul throughout all its lives on this plane.

The Ten Soul Ages

The young soul chain:

- The Level 1 soul
- The Level 2 soul
- The Level 3 soul
- The Level 4 soul
- The Level 5 soul

The old soul chain:

- The Level 6 soul
- The Level 7 soul
- The Level 8 soul
- The Level 9 soul
- The Level 10 soul

As we progress through each level, we learn lessons that are appropriate for the experience of our soul. As we battle with the Illusion, we learn to overcome the risk and embrace the advantage associated with each stage of our soul's growth.

Advantages, Risks, and the Illusion

The Illusion is, quite simply, the belief that what you see is all there is—that life begins and ends on the Physical Plane.

Risks are the result of ignoring your soul's guidance, and prevent you from experiencing everything your soul wants you to in your lifetime.

Living the life your soul intended requires that you break through the barrier of the Illusion. The way to do that is to follow your soul's guidance by embracing the advantage associated with each element of the Instruction.

Every single person on the planet has the ability to overcome the Illusion. They simply have to want to.

As it makes its way through its many lifetimes, the soul gradually casts aside the Illusion to overcome fear and self-interest. Each lifetime builds on the successes and failures of the last, until we finally learn that love and understanding are the forces that unite us.

Young Souls

The Level 1 Soul
Advantage: Identification
Risk: Apprehension

In their first few lives, Level 1 souls deliberately avoid having to deal with the modern world. They feel apprehensive about being on a planet where everyone seems to know the rules but them.

They usually choose to live in small communities where they can avoid complexity. In simple cultures, these novice souls learn to take their first steps, often through learning trades or skills that will support them.

The Level 1 Need for Simplicity

The Level 1 soul is easily overwhelmed by technology and complexity. You wouldn't take a three-year-old from a remote farm in Idaho, place it on the corner of fourteenth and third in downtown Manhattan, and expect it to know how to safely cross the street.

Nor can you transport a Level 1 soul from the simplicity of an isolated village and expect it to fit into the rough and tumble of corporate life on Wall Street.

Level 1 souls create rules and rituals that give them a sense of security. It's all part of learning what it is to be human.

The advantage associated with being a Level 1 soul is identification: learning to see yourself as an individual and, at the same time, discovering the importance of belonging to a culture. Shared beliefs, values, and codes of behavior are an essential part of the Level 1 education. The risk at this level is apprehension, where a fear of being on the Physical Plane can cause many of these very young souls to withdraw from the world.

Level 1 souls are generally poor at using language because it's so new to them. Their literature, their art, and their understanding of the world tend to be extremely limited.

But by the time they've completed this level (and that might take several lifetimes), they'll be ready to handle more complex lessons about cooperating and sharing with others.

The Level 2 Soul
Advantage: Cooperation
Risk: Mistrust

Level 2 souls are less afraid of the world than they were in their first few lifetimes. Still, they prefer not to take any chances. They protect themselves with AK-47s, draconian laws, and vengeful gods. They see the world in terms of black and white, them and us, and good and evil. Their fundamentalism and obedience to authority helps them avoid facing what might be uncomfortable questions.

Being relatively new to the world makes these inexperienced souls easily taken advantage of. In the past, carpetbaggers would prey on them. These days, they end up being suckered by politicians who ship their jobs overseas while promising to keep them safe from terrorists, immigrants, gays, and other distractions and scapegoats.

By deliberately disconnecting themselves from the mainstream, Level 2 souls can get used to being on the Physical Plane without fear of running into the kind of opposing views that might threaten their rigid beliefs. For this reason, they tend to choose to live in rural areas or small towns where they can learn this level's advantage: the importance of cooperation with others.

They create strict laws, usually wrapped up in religious language, to help keep them on the straight and narrow. Only their God is the true God, and everyone else will perish in hell or be refused entrance to the afterlife.

Since their experience is too narrow to allow them to understand other souls, Level 2 souls assume that those who don't subscribe to the same rigid codes of behavior lack a moral compass.

And because other souls don't see the world like they do, those "others" must be bad. And if they're bad, they must be punished— which is why Level 2 souls use the courts to legislate morality. The world's prisons are packed with those whose crimes are victimless but offend Level 2 sensibilities. They include prostitutes, drug users, homosexuals, blasphemers, and political dissenters.

Mistrust of others (the risk) is at its peak at Level 2, which makes it hard to attain genuine intimacy, and leads to a discomfort with sex. It's their belief that human desires are not something to be enjoyed—they're dirty and shameful.

Since Level 2 souls lack experience, they can't begin to understand those unlike themselves. They perceive huge gulfs between races, religions, and genders. Their men regard themselves as better than women, whose place is very much in the home. (Very young souls equate physical strength with superiority.)

Misogyny

Depending on how much they're wrapped up in the Illusion, and the kind of society in which they live, younger-soul men will find different ways of expressing their fear of women by subjugating them. They jail prostitutes, stone adulteresses, mandate female circumcision, refuse girls an education, and deny contraception or the opportunity to terminate a pregnancy.

In many societies, Level 2 women assist in their own subjugation because of their belief that they should be subservient to men.

The genuine recognition that men and women are equal doesn't come until after the soul graduates to become an old soul.

Throughout history, those Level 2 souls who are most in thrall to the Illusion have tried to clamp down on what they fear or don't understand: Elvis, blue jeans, the corrupting influence of other cultures, marijuana, civil rights, equal rights, sex toys, pornography, contraception, conflicting religions, gay rights, alcohol, rap music, and freedom of speech.

It will be a long time before they learn to live and let live.

The Level 3 Soul

Advantage: Belonging
Risk: Conformity

Level 3 souls tend to act emotionally rather than rationally. They'll buy a truck because they believe it's the "Heartbeat of America." It doesn't matter that it's actually made in Canada or Mexico.

These souls want to belong (the advantage), whether it's as part of the family or the nation. They create strong families, which they glue together with firm religious beliefs and strict moral codes.

Their real need is to fit into their community, and as they do this they often slip into the risk, which is conformity. A Level 3 soul would never let their lawn become overgrown with weeds and stand out from everyone else's. And they're attracted to places like mega-churches where they can blend in and feel part of the majority.

Few things escape Level 3 souls more than a protestor in a foreign country burning the Stars and Stripes. They see it as a sign of the utmost contempt.

In the US, younger souls have fought for decades to keep the Confederate flag flying over the South Carolina statehouse. For Level 2 and 3 souls, wherever they happen to be, the flag is a vitally important symbol of their own identity, which is why they refuse to surrender it without a fight.

At Level 3, there is still a need for safety and reassurance. Thanks to the influence of these souls, recently published books reveal that the Grand Canyon was formed not five to six million years ago, as science would have it, but in the last few thousand years. Creationism offers a kind of certainty that can't be found in complex scientific theories.

Level 3 souls' lives are more urban than those in the previous stages. They develop well-functioning, though insular, societies, where the trains always run on time, and everyone can enjoy the benefits of belonging to a community—providing they fit in.

Work hard, go to a socially approved place of worship, be a good citizen, and everything will be fine.

Contradict the community's beliefs, upset the status quo, or step out of line, and you're in trouble. That's because conformity, and the safety it offers, is so vitally important to them.

Like those at the previous level, these souls are still a little uncomfortable with intimacy. Their focus is very much outward. And because they don't look within for answers, they place the blame for life's ills on scapegoats: single mothers, welfare cheats, immigrants, and gays.

Young souls, particularly those at Level 3, are drawn to nationalism (something they confuse with patriotism). Their country, whichever one it happens to be, is the greatest nation on earth. And since they identify with their country, which they see as a reflection of themselves, its strength becomes their strength.

Political and military leaders, who are most often at Level 5, have always exploited this trait to gain support for military or imperialistic ventures. Level 3 souls have traditionally marched off to war, whistling patriotic songs, convinced that dying for their country is an honor.

Dulce et Decorum Est

You might think, given the way younger souls tend to be more willing than older souls to march into battle, that they have no fear of death.

In fact, they have a great deal of fear connected with death. One way they control the fear is through a belief in a glorious afterlife, where they'll be rewarded for their bravery.

Vikings created a complex mythology surrounding death. Slain warriors, it was believed, would spend eternity in Valhalla, where they'd be treated as heroes.

Level 3 souls believe that certain individuals are innately superior to others. They revere monarchs, presidents, and religious figures (as long as they feel their values are being respected).

Thanks to a belief in their own inferiority and the need to belong, Level 3 souls who are disadvantaged gain solidarity from being around others who are equally disadvantaged. Those who break out of this conformity can be threatening. If one of them flies too high and crashes back to ground, they'll be held up as an example of someone who forgot their place in the natural order of things.

The Level 4 Soul

Advantage: Expansion

Risk: Hypocrisy

By the time the soul graduates to Level 4, it has begun to lose much of the awkwardness and discomfort it once felt so acutely. It starts to get much more involved in the running of things. Like a little kid trying to join in a game with bigger kids, the Level 4 soul wants to emulate those he or she looks up to.

And that would be those at the next level. Like a cool older brother, Level 5 souls are comfortable in their own skins and understand the rules of the game. In contrast, Level 4 souls are conscious of their own lack of sophistication. Still, this level is all about achieving the advantage: expansion. These souls are going to put themselves out into the bigger world whether they're ready or not.

Level 4 souls make a big impact on their offspring. Their own desire to achieve makes them committed parents. They want their children to do well, in part because their successes will reflect well on Mom and Dad, but also because at this level they're starting to recognize that their children are unique individuals, not simply extensions of themselves.

This is a difficult stage. Behind them, they have the morality of younger souls, and ahead is the often unabashed materialism of Level 5.

As they try awkwardly to straddle both God and Mammon, they often fall into the risk, hypocrisy, where their lack of worldly experience shows itself.

They'll rail at others for their moral failings, but will later be found to have a gambling problem, drug addiction, or an illegitimate child. When they get busted, their tendency is to deny they have a problem or blame the media ("they took my words out of context"), their political opponents ("I'm the victim of a smear campaign"), or their past beliefs ("I used to be a sinner, but now I'm born again").

Whipping Boys

During their childhood years, many European kings had a whipping boy, a servant who'd take a beating for his young master's failings in the classroom.

Level 4 souls often find a whipping boy to punish for crimes they themselves have committed (even if they're not crimes in anyone's eyes but their own). It helps them exorcise their feelings of guilt or shame.

In recent years, a Level 4 soul mayor of the city of Spokane, Washington, spent much of his career opposing gay rights. He sponsored a bill that not only called for gays and lesbians to be barred from jobs in schools and day-care centers, but would also have had them fired simply for being gay or lesbian.

Then he was caught surfing the net for male companionship. He'd tried to trade sex in exchange for a government job, and ended up losing his own.

The Level 4 mayor's whipping boys were gays—in whom he saw his own "failings" reflected back at him.

As they begin to branch out into the world, Level 4 souls build strong communities and take a greater-than-ever interest in education and developing particular careers. They're looking for specific lessons that will help them survive in the competitive world of Level 5.

The Level 5 Soul
Advantage: Exploration
Risk: Exploitation

Level 5 souls are exciting, dynamic, and always striving to push things forward. If it weren't for them, we'd probably all still be traveling by horse and cart.

Level 5 souls fully embrace the world. In fact, they believe it's theirs for the taking. The uncertainty of younger soul ages is replaced by a feeling of self-assurance. They roam the world with confidence, determined to make their mark and their fortune in equal measure as they investigate the advantage: exploration.

The grip of the Illusion is at its strongest at this level. Genuine spiritual awakening may still be possible, but it will take great effort to achieve. For many, the Spiritual Plane is about as real as Neverland.

For those who are wrapped up in the Illusion, the risk or downside of their ambition is exploitation. Their tendency is to take what they want, regardless of the long-term consequences.

The courage of their convictions inspires a belief in the civilizing effects of imperialism. Throughout history, they've conquered other societies to bring them the benefits of a more technological and, in their eyes, a more advanced culture.

Level 5 souls love the excitement of politics, with all its opportunities for self-advancement and intrigue. Yet those of them who are most in thrall to the Illusion don't want to govern so much as rule. Even if their country is at war, the real enemy is always the opposition party (if one is tolerated).

And when it comes to war, they find it a great way to express their power. Their leaders send mighty armies to battle the mighty armies of other Level 5 leaders in the belief that the answer to violence is more violence. They equate belligerence with power, which they don't clearly distinguish from strength. And because the opposite of strength is weakness, and they fear being seen as weak, they feel it's important to act tough.

The Fear of Appearing Weak

After a US Navy warship shot down an Iranian passenger plane, killing 290 civilians, Level 5 former president George H. W. Bush said, "I will never apologize for the United States, ever. I don't care what the facts are."

His comments reflect the Level 5 soul's strength of conviction and fear of weakness, and also a lack of connection that comes from being fully immersed in the Illusion.

Even though aggressors have a poor chance of actually winning a war, the Illusion prevents many young souls from learning from experience or from the past. They'll invade another country in the belief that the war will be over in weeks, or that they'll be greeted with open arms. The lessons of history are lost on them.

Level 5 souls build great cities that buzz with activity. And because they're always pushing forward, technology advances at breathtaking speed. Their thirst for novelty guarantees that a market will always be there for new products.

Power: The Level 5 Soul Aphrodisiac

Each soul age has its own particular focus. At the end of the young soul chain, the soul is learning all about exploration. Part of this lesson is about wielding power.

Power in itself is such an attraction that Level 5 souls will often accept a significant drop in income in exchange for a job with more status and the opportunity to exert greater power and influence.

Wall Street is a Level 5 soul invention, as are massive corporations. They appeal to the Level 5 soul's desire to make an impact on the world. (It should be pointed out, however, that souls of all ages end up working for these organizations.)

From Alexander the Great to most US presidents, virtually every world leader has been a Level 5 soul. All of them have created change, both good and bad, welcome and unwelcome. They're the reason political boundaries are continually changing.

These souls have little time for introspection—that won't come until they graduate to the next level. And they still have the young soul tendency to isolate themselves. In this case, they do it by building gated communities and apartment blocks that limit social interaction.

Face lifts and boob jobs are the Level 5 soul's way of prolonging youth. The underlying belief is that old age equals death, and young souls have a fear of their own mortality that won't dissipate until they're well into the next level.

Old Souls

The Level 6 Soul

Advantage: Introspection
Risk: Self-Doubt

At the point souls evolve from young to old, they undergo a 180-degree flip as their focus shifts from exploring outward to exploring inward. This search for the meaning of life is called the Quest, and will last from the beginning of Level 6 until their final lifetime on Earth at the end of Level 10.

The Quest

The Quest is the pursuit of self-knowledge. It begins with the desire to understand the purpose of life and gradually transforms into a desire to understand the purpose of one particular life: your own.

Instead of accepting conventional wisdom, Level 6 souls question everything. Thanks to the shift in perspective, the guilelessness of earlier soul ages is replaced with skepticism. They begin to see that the world isn't quite the place those in authority tell them it is.

When their souls were much younger, they used to put up with injustice in the belief that they'd get their reward in the hereafter.

Now they're not so compliant.

They want more fairness for themselves and those around them, and they want it in this life, not the next. For that reason, they form trade unions, cooperatives, and other organizations that offer mutual support.

Level 6 souls begin to find materialism shallow, yet they're not sure where happiness does lie. They sense a need for deeper meaning in their lives. They may even describe themselves as spiritual rather than religious.

They explore themselves through literature and art. (They are creative, though rarely innovative.) Other people become fascinating creatures, and learning what makes them tick helps Level 6 souls learn what they, themselves, are all about.

The fear that once made them wary of those who appear different begins to lessen its grip. Having reincarnated many times in a variety of races and cultures helps them to develop acceptance. It also helps them to lose the fear of death that afflicts so many younger souls.

Thanks to the Quest, and their newfound introspection (this level's advantage), instead of looking for problems outside of themselves they look inward, often creating mountains out of their own personal molehills. And thanks to the risk, self-doubt, they'll suffer deep conflicts over issues such as their spiritual beliefs or sexual orientation.

As the Illusion takes a less prominent role in their lives, they gravitate toward pacifism. Discomfort with armed conflict begins at Level 6. There are two reasons.

The first is that multiple lifetimes on the battlefield teach older souls about the futility of war. The second is that the introspection that begins at this level creates a dawning awareness that we humans are actually all connected.

As this consciousness grows, Level 6 souls lose the will to rule and dominate. They see that diplomacy and cooperation are actually the best way to have their needs met.

By the time they leave this stage of their development behind, these souls will have gained the insight necessary to take them into Level 7.

The Level 7 Soul

Advantage: Innovation
Risk: Anxiety

Young-soul drive and old-soul introspection collide at Level 7, resulting in spectacular achievements. Great inventions are created, masterpieces are painted, and new discoveries are made. Level 7 Souls brought us aviation (the Wright brothers), the Sistine Chapel (Michelangelo), and penicillin (Alexander Fleming).

Innovative Level 7 souls played huge roles in the Renaissance, the ages of discovery and enlightenment, and many medical and technological breakthroughs. In fact, innovation is the advantage at Level 7.

Never before or after this stage will they be quite so creative, inventive, or curious. Their drive will diminish from this point on.

Having fully embraced the Quest, they can be self-absorbed to the point where neurosis sets in. Angst-ridden poets and artists appear, all of them looking for the meaning of something: art, literature, and particularly life itself.

These souls are unfamiliar with self-analysis, yet they do their best, writing complex philosophies that make life seem much more complicated than it is.

They feel the need to continually further their understanding of the world. This urge, combined with the desire to help each other, results in the creation of societies and organizations dedicated to the pursuit of knowledge.

One Percent Inspiration

The great inventor Thomas Edison had the energy and drive of a young soul. But, in fact, he was at Level 7, and that's what gave him the ability to tap into inspiration from the Soul World.

One of Edison's more old-soul habits was to hold small brass balls in his hands while he went into a meditative state. Just as he reached that point between being awake and asleep, his grip would relax, he'd drop the balls, and the noise would wake him up. Then he'd write down the inspired thoughts that came to him.

He claimed that "genius is one percent inspiration and 99 percent perspiration." That 1 percent came from the other side.

It may interest you to know that Edison's last words were, "It's very beautiful over there." Was he referring to the view from his bedroom window, or did he catch a glimpse of a world beyond?

At this level, the world becomes more fascinating than ever before, thanks to a dimension that was previously missing: inner complexity.

Level 7 souls discover unplumbed depths within themselves. Tortured artists look for other tortured souls so they won't feel quite so alone. They find it exciting to be in the presence of those who share their passion for discussion and analysis.

Insecurity and great art and music go hand in hand because so many artists and musicians are, or were, at this level. Impressionist painter Édouard Manet and composer Ludwig van Beethoven are typical examples of angst-ridden genius. The Impressionists were almost all Level 7 souls. And, like many groups of artists before and since, they struggled with the purpose of life and the meaning of art.

The consequence of all this intensity and drama can be a kind of sensory overload. Anxiety (the risk) ensues, preventing these souls from achieving whatever it was they originally set out to do.

What unites Level 7 souls is a love of life's luxuries, particularly good food and wine. They take a great interest in the arts of all kind, and are especially drawn to whatever breaks new ground.

The Level 8 Soul

Advantage: Reciprocity
Risk: Complacency

Level 8 souls are fully immersed in their lives. They have emotionally intense relationships that allow them to explore their multifaceted inner worlds.

They admire creativity but, unlike Level 7 souls, they're more likely to be patrons of the arts than actually artists.

At Level 8, the growing comprehension that we're all one results in far greater concern for others. The advantage at this level is reciprocity, where the need to learn the ins and outs of mutual dependence drives them to create a better world.

They get involved in politics and socially conscious charities, and seek out groups of people who, like them, want the world to be a better place. You can find them in progressive political parties, Amnesty International, Doctors Without Borders, and Greenpeace. And though these organizations attract all kinds of souls, from Level 5 onward, it's Level 8 souls who tend to participate the most.

Level 8 souls run the risk of complacency. It can happen when they join a group or committee. They put in lots of work, get heavily involved in the process, but ultimately change nothing. The fire in the belly that once made them highly driven younger souls is, by now, more of a smoldering ember. Sometimes they'll forget that it's not all about the journey—there are goals to achieve too.

Most Level 8 souls recycle and drive cars that contribute the least to global warming—traits that will last until they leave the Physical Plane at the end of Level 10. They want to create a pleasant living environment for themselves and others. (And that includes future residents of planet Earth.)

Lifetimes of experience have taught them that there is really no difference between people of different ethnic groups or genders. As the Illusion wears thin, even those who are fully immersed in it can't avoid becoming more intensely connected to the Soul World. They begin to seek out peaceful solutions to conflicts, both personal and national.

With many dramatic incarnations behind them, Level 8 souls want to be left alone to live their lives in their own way. Their biggest fear is that they'll have their lives disrupted in some way—by government intrusion, war, or invasion, for example.

The Level 9 Soul

Advantage: Self-Improvement

Risk: Preoccupation

Level 9 is a time to work on personal issues: confronting phobias, overcoming addictions, and correcting flaws.

Whether they know it or not, these senior-citizen souls are all working on issues from past lives. With so much grief and heartache behind them, many will spend a lifetime in therapy or finding ways to understand their emotional side.

As the Illusion loses its grip, spirituality gains immense importance. Now that they're nearing Level 10, and with it their last few lifetimes on the Physical Plane, Level 9 souls develop a greater-than-ever consciousness that we're all connected to each other.

They seek out faiths in which they feel comfortable, rather than the church they grew up in. Buddhism and contemplative practices allow them to connect to the universe in a profound way.

Spiritual Exploration

Level 9 souls like to explore their spirituality in intimate groups rather than huge places of worship. They're attracted to retreats where they feel safe investigating themselves in the company of like-minded souls, often members of their own sex.

There are debts from previous lives that must be repaid, or at least worked on. (Level 9 souls don't want to leave this penultimate level with unfinished business behind them.) They may spend several lifetimes completing lessons and balancing experiences to tie up loose ends from previous incarnations.

The advantage is self-improvement. The risk, however, is that Level 9 souls may become totally preoccupied with their own issues to the exclusion of more worldly concerns, like their careers or even their families.

Despite their advancing age, Level 9 souls still have some drive left in them. They'll sometimes end up in the corporate world. And when they do (like Ben and Jerry), they'll do their best to create ethical businesses with quality products. They'll support charities and find ways to leave the world a better place.

The Level 10 Soul

Advantage: Compassion
Risk: Passivity

At Level 10, the soul is ready for retirement. Conventional ideas of success become meaningless. Materialism becomes less important than ever. Who cares about making money if you've got to be part of the rat race to do it?

There is a slightly lower level of self-absorption, now that the intense healing work of Level 9 is behind them. Most live quiet lives, doing work they love, in the hope it will contribute to society.

They can be highly talented but lacking in drive or ambition. Those around them may feel that they never quite reach their potential. The risk at this level is passivity. These easygoing souls have many lifetimes of achievement behind them, and often develop a sense of having been there and done it all before.

Sometimes a Level 10 soul will abandon a successful career to focus on something that interests them, even if it means a huge drop in income or status.

Level 10 souls usually don't stand out as being anything unusual. More than any other souls, they're likely to ignore prevailing fashions and go their own way. They might shop in the local Goodwill store—even if they can afford designer labels. Most people who are genuinely eccentric are Level 10 souls.

Clusters of Souls

Souls of a particular age will be drawn to certain countries or cities for the mutual lessons they hope to explore. That's why whole regions can be identified as being of a specific soul age.

Norway, for example, is a predominantly Level 10 country. It has a strong social infrastructure and is unlikely to ever go to war against its neighbors.

Their focus is on expressing compassion (the advantage) and learning to be both physical and spiritual. Having compassion requires them to be very much part of the physical world in order that others can receive their love. As long as they can receive love in return, Level 10 souls can be happy just about anywhere (though they generally prefer tranquility over noise).

Altruism is at its peak at Level 10. With lifetimes of experience behind them, these souls see another person suffering and remember when they, too, were in that same situation.

As each lifetime takes them closer to returning to the Universal Consciousness, the Illusion becomes increasingly easy to overcome. They have, to some degree, the awareness that all of humanity is connected and deserving of respect. They can see the folly of war, the shallowness of unbridled materialism, and the dangers of unregulated power.

Old-Soul Altruism

Dorothy and Gwen Hennessey are sister-sisters, Franciscan nuns who are also birth sisters. At the ages of eighty-eight and sixty-eight, respectively, they were arrested and sentenced to six months each for protesting outside the notorious School of the Americas in Georgia. The school, renamed the Western Hemisphere Institute for Security, is where soldiers from foreign countries come to learn torture techniques.

Neither Dorothy nor Gwen faces the slightest risk of being tortured in a foreign country themselves. They put their freedom on the line to help people they'll never meet.

As Level 10 souls, they know in their hearts that we're all one.

At this advanced age, the soul's connection to others makes killing unacceptable. Level 10 souls oppose war, the death penalty, and torture.

Like peace activist Cindy Sheehan and Kathy Kelly, founder of Voices in the Wilderness (both Level 10 souls who have been jailed for their opposition to violence), they may, in their last few lifetimes, become outspoken advocates for peace and justice.

Old souls like these are frightening to younger souls who are caught up in the Illusion, and they risk derision and even imprisonment for their actions. They often end up with huge FBI files that speak volumes about the way concepts like peace, freedom, fairness, and justice are really viewed by the younger-soul establishment.

Where Does the Self-Interest Go?

The soul's journey, as I previously mentioned, takes it from a state of self-interest to altruism: selfless concern for the well-being of others.

Let me pose this question: what happens to the self-interest? In other words, where does it go?

I'll give you the answer at the end of the book.

Level 10 souls, like most older souls, respect the environment, knowing that future generations will have to live with the planet we leave behind.

Their philosophies are uncomplicated and cut directly to the chase. Experience has taught them the profound nature of simple statements like "all you need is love," "an eye for an eye makes the whole world blind," and "treat others as you'd have them treat you."

Determine Your Own Soul Age

Now that we've explored each of the ten soul ages, it's time to figure out where you fit into the great scheme of things.

Begin by entering a meditative state (you might want to refer to the section on meditation on page 14), then call in your spirit guides. Ask them for their help in determining your soul age.

Use the ten brief descriptions to help remind you of the focus of each level. Try not to over-analyze. Trust your intuition.

Level 1: Isolation, Apprehension, Simplicity, Naivety
Level 2: Fundamentalism, Nationalism, Conservatism,
  Discrimination

Level 3: Church, Community, Conservatism, Conformity

Level 4: Religion, Aspiration, Morality, Conservatism

Level 5: Ambition, Materialism, Power, Mainstream Views

Level 6: Unity, Social Justice, Drama, Self-questioning

Level 7: Complexity, Curiosity, Creativity, Intensity

Level 8: Sophistication, Liberalism, Environmentalism, Activism

Level 9: Spirituality, Self-improvement, Healing, Idealism

Level 10: Altruism, Connection, Eccentricity, Inertia

Soul Age: _____

Ask your spirit guides to support you in manifesting your soul age.
Repeat the following:

*"I call upon my Causal spirit guides, acting in my highest interest,
to help me manifest my soul age to allow me to live the life my soul
intended."*

When you've finished, thank your spirit guides and tell them,
"Session over."

• • •

The soul age has a profound impact on how you see the world. No
matter how old you are in years, it's your soul's experience that will
have the greatest effect on your beliefs and behavior.

Yet there is clearly more to who you are than just your soul age.

That's why, next, we're going to take a journey back in time, to
explore an event that created our wondrous diversity and ensured
that each of us would be born into the world with an acute sense of
our own individuality.

3: THE DOOR TO ACCEPTANCE
Soul Types: The Heart of Your Individuality

Prior to ensoulment, Homo sapiens *understood little*
of the world around them. They lived in tribes with social structures
resembling that of gorillas, in which each day was almost
indistinguishable from the one before.
—THE AUTHOR'S CAUSAL GUIDES

People who think babies are born as blank slates can't ever have met one. They show signs of their individuality as soon as they're born. Some of them are placid; others turn diaper-changing into a martial art. One will be demanding and clingy, the next will get on just fine without you.

The reason is that each one of us brings a complete personality into this world. The moment we hit the ground, however, everyone tries to change us. Even the most well-meaning parents will want to mold their offspring in some way.

A sensitive boy is told to toughen up. A dominant girl learns that nice girls don't act that way. Rather than risk losing Mom and Dad's acceptance, they'll simply become something they're not.

Very often, by the time you're grown up, your soul-level personality will have been buried beneath a personality of your own creation, one based on others' expectations.

The Door to Acceptance takes you to a place where you can reclaim the personality you were born with by uncovering the source of your individuality: your soul type.

The result will be profound self-acceptance. And that will lead to everything from inner peace to the confidence to make better choices by knowing what's best for you.

To help you understand the source of your personality, this part of the journey is going to take you back to a time, somewhere around fifty-five thousand years ago, when Homo sapiens first got souls.

Before this event, life for early humans was dull and monotonous. The pace of development was so slow that one generation looked just like the last.

We lived in tribes made up of several hundred individuals, which gave us protection as well as insurance against inbreeding. Infant mortality was high, and the chance of surviving beyond the age of thirty was slim.

Though we'd learned to cook, we suffered from the effects of parasitic disease and other food-borne ailments. The problem was that cooking wasn't done regularly or effectively, and we often ate carrion and unsafe meat. Then, as now, many of us developed osteoarthritis and heart disease.

The Purpose of the Appendix

Our ancestors had diets that contained everything from gravel to bits of bone and gristle. Fortunately, they had a well-functioning appendix, which helped break down blockages in the large intestine.

Our concerns were simply to do with survival: getting enough to eat, staying warm, and avoiding wild animals. We had fire, which gave us some comfort as well as protection from the elements. And, after many thousands of years, we'd learned to use very simple stone tools.

Then, in the space of a single generation, something radical happened. In a process called ensoulment, every member of our species was given a soul.

We would never be the same again.

• • •

At this point, I'd like to stop and digress. I'm often asked questions like "Does Fluffy have a soul?" and "Are there other species with souls on the planet?"

The answer is yes. But to understand the difference between Fluffy and you, it's important to know a little about the nature of consciousness.

On the Physical Plane, there are three stages of consciousness. A creature at the first stage will operate almost entirely on an instinctive level. A rat, for example, is conscious enough to know it is alive, yet its ability to make choices is extremely limited. It will always behave in a rat-like way.

A bee functions entirely instinctively, and therefore shows no sign of having creative thought. It will sting without considering the consequences to itself or its unfortunate victim.

The second stage of consciousness is seen in dogs, cats, and other large mammals. Most are able to exercise some degree of choice. They can weigh certain options and reach conclusions. If it's raining, a cat can decide whether to go out on the prowl or stay indoors. When it makes a choice like this, an animal is displaying signs of elevated consciousness.

The third stage of consciousness is found in humans and cetaceans (whales, dolphins, and porpoises), and is marked by the ability to make complex choices.

Fluffy, like any animal at stage two, can't have her consciousness elevated by being brought into a stage three environment. She's never going to learn to read, no matter how much we help her. Those at stage three, however, can be taught highly complex tasks.

Stage one and two creatures are guided by a collective consciousness that's specific to their particular species. This consciousness resides on the Astral Plane, making it easily accessible to them.

My spirit guides use the term "ensoulment" to describe elevation from stage two to stage three. Which is precisely what happened to us fifty-five thousand years ago.

• • •

With billions of souls and potential host species in the universe, why did our souls choose us, *Homo sapiens?* Why not gorillas or our nearest competitors, Neanderthals, who had coexisted alongside us for more than one hundred thousand years?

These are just some of the qualities that first attracted our souls to our species:

- Large numbers to help ensure long-term survival
- Potentially long life expectancy
- Tongues and palates that allowed us to form words
- Large brains with the potential for growth
- The ability to walk on two legs to free up our hands
- Agility to make us good hunters
- Three-dimensional vision
- Opposable thumbs

At the time we were given souls, there was really no other serious contender. Neanderthals were physically strong and shared a lot of our abilities. They could make tools, light a fire, and communicate in a rudimentary way. Resources were plentiful and there was little competition between *Homo sapiens* and Neanderthals. Unfortunately, the Neanderthals were sick with a disease similar to the one we know as chlamydia. Starting around thirty thousand years ago, infertility, a side effect of the disease, eventually caused them to die out completely.

What exactly did having a soul do for our species? Here are some of the most significant developments:

- Abstract thought
- Beliefs
- The ability to understand symbols and metaphors
- Curiosity
- New ways to learn
- Problem-solving skills
- Distinct emotions
- Imagination
- Creativity
- Sense of humor

Once we had souls, we had abstract thought, and that sparked a sudden evolutionary surge forward. We left the other primates in the dust. We learned to cook properly, build shelter, and make better tools using bones, antlers, and wood, instead of just stone. Improved weapons led to more sophisticated hunting techniques, which in turn gave us more to eat.

With better nutrition and protection from the elements, health improved. Longevity increased. And that gave us more reproductive years. Very quickly the population exploded.

This sudden growth in numbers suited our souls. The more of us there were, the higher our chances of survival as a species. The higher our chances of succeeding as a species, the greater the opportunity for our souls to learn about being human.

It was in how we learned that some of the biggest changes could be seen. We began learning from our mistakes, from watching others and from past experience.

And our children began to learn through play. It was a serious business. They did it to learn how to survive, not just for fun.

Imagine watching a child crawling on all fours, grunting like a pig, and another making lunging movements with a stick. We'd figure out almost immediately that one was pretending to be a hunter and the other an animal. But this strange behavior would have made no sense at all to pre-ensoulment humans. All they'd have seen would have been one child waving a stick and another on all fours. That's because they lacked one of the most striking features of ensoulment: the ability to understand metaphors.

Understanding metaphors gave rise to cave paintings—the means to relate a flat image on a cave wall to a real, live animal somewhere else. And it allowed us to tell our children fables: stories that rely on metaphors.

There was something else the soul brought us: the ability to imagine, anticipate, and predict. We could use these skills to picture an object before we created it, learn to take shelter before it rained, and figure out that spring followed winter.

Humans had never known jealousy before. But with ensoulment, we suddenly had the ability to compare and contrast. And once we could do that, we could see ourselves in relation to others.

Comparing and contrasting led to resentment, envy, feelings of superiority, arrogance, low self-esteem, humility, and a host of other emotions we'd never previously had. But it also helped us develop an enhanced sense of our own individuality and gave us something that helped transform us into who we are today: distinct personality types.

For the first time, jobs were chosen based on ability instead of gender or age. It became obvious that some members of the tribe made excellent hunters while others couldn't throw a spear to save their lives. So it dawned on us that those with less physical strength might be put to better use carrying water or tending the fire.

In the past, our tribes had been led by the dominant males. Now we expected something more than brute strength in our leaders. Strength was still important, but courage and wisdom were also recognized as worthy qualifications.

We still find individuals among us with natural leadership skills. John F. Kennedy was a tribal chief whose tribe just happened to number almost 200 million.

And though our hunters no longer run around hurling spears at woolly mammoths, they still retain the qualities that made them good at what they did: they're task-oriented and physically active.

The artists in our modern tribes are still responsible for the creativity that moves us on a soul level. Most visual artists are the spiritual descendants of the creative geniuses who first learned to apply ground pigment and charcoal to the walls of their caves. Steven Spielberg, for example, expresses himself in a medium that's simply a contemporary equivalent of cave painting.

Creatures of Reason

There are ten soul types, each of which is named after its original purpose in the tribe. Every one of us has a central soul type that is the core of who we are. And then we have the influence of two of the other nine types.

Your soul type may change from one lifetime to the next, but you'll generally have a favorite—one you tend to stick to. Most of us choose from the three we're most comfortable with. This is one of the reasons a soul will explore themes, such as teaching or creativity, over many successive lifetimes.

The Ten Soul Types

- The Helper type
- The Caregiver type
- The Educator type
- The Thinker type
- The Creator type
- The Performer type
- The Hunter type
- The Leader type
- The Spiritualist type
- The Transformer type

Though your soul type will always be the most significant part of who you are, the influence will affect how you express your individuality.

Soul-type Influences

- Soul type: behavior plus traits
- Primary influence: behavior
- Secondary influence: traits

Your soul type gives you both the behavior and trait associated with a particular type. If you're a Creator type, you'll have creativity, the behavior, and sensitivity and idealism, the strongest traits.

If your primary influence is the Thinker type, you'll have the behavior but not the traits. You'll be analytical and want to accumulate knowledge, but you'll lack the Thinker restraint.

And if your secondary influence is that of a Performer type, you'll have passion, the trait, but you're unlikely to have a burning desire to see your name in lights on Broadway.

The advantage associated with your soul type is attained by following your soul's guidance. It allows you to express who you are positively, and prevents you from slipping into the risk, which, in every case, is the result of ignoring your soul's influence.

In my sessions with clients, I always look for a soul type and two influences. It helps to create a more complete picture. I realize, however, that this may be asking a lot of you. If you can identify your soul type and one influence, you'll be doing well. But if you feel adventurous enough, try looking for that second influence as well.

Let's now start at the beginning and explore the ten basic soul types.

The Helper Type
Advantage: Service
Risk: Submission

When Emma arrived in my office, she was close to tears. "I feel totally overwhelmed," she told me.

It turned out she'd just agreed to deliver five hundred leaflets door to door, even though her job and her charity work left her with no spare time that month.

"I can't say no," she said.

I wasn't particularly surprised. Emma is a Helper type. The desire to assist others comes directly from her soul. It was clear that she was an old soul, struggling against the effects of the risk, which, in this case, is submission. I told her she wasn't alone. All over the world there are Helpers who get themselves into this kind of mess.

"I've always been this way," she sighed. "I'm always the one who ends up agreeing to arrange the flowers at church or take care of someone's dog."

Helpers like Emma need someone or something to be of service to. And that's something they can do pretty much anywhere. There are Helpers in the fields of medicine and science, and there are Helpers who are janitors and shop assistants. The entire emergency team at the scene of an accident may be Helper types.

They bring common sense and stability to the world. They are stable, stoic, and will simply get on with their work without fuss.

Their inherent dedication assists them in applying themselves to a task. And their stoicism is the reason they'll put in forty years of unstinting service in a thankless job, taking pride in never having missed a day's work due to sickness.

Unfortunately, other people will recognize their desire to help and take advantage of it. Who can you ask to do the job no one else wants to do? The Helper, of course.

But what of Emma? What was the solution to her problem? It was to recognize that by getting pulled in lots of different directions, she wasn't helping anyone. She had no time for her family or herself, and the jobs she'd taken on couldn't be done to anyone's satisfaction, including her own.

By the end of the session, Emma had been guided to set boundaries, and to ask herself whether she was taking on tasks because she wanted to or because she felt pressured into doing so.

As she left, I couldn't help teasing her a little. "I have two hundred envelopes to address and mail by tomorrow morning," I said. "Do you think you could help?"

Emma looked at me and stammered, "I . . . uh . . . oh, well, maybe . . . " Then she realized I was joking. "I mean no! Absolutely not! No way!" she said boldly.

I gave her a hug and said, "Good job!"

The Caregiver Type

Advantage: Nurture
Risk: Self-Neglect

This soul type is here to nurture and, as the name suggests, take care of others. Caregivers make committed parents, nurses, nannies, and careworkers, and they may end up looking after an aging or sickly relative as a way of expressing themselves. For Caregivers, such work is rarely a chore—it comes straight from the soul.

I asked Jan, a preschool teacher, if she'd always recognized her nurturing trait. She said, "I was always kind-hearted and good to animals, but it was only in my late twenties, when I began caring for foster children and then had kids of my own, that it really kicked in.

"After that, I totally accepted who I am. I realized that I'm a giving person—I have a lot of empathy and sensitivity."

"Have you ever found it overwhelming to be taking care of others all the time?" I asked.

"Oh, yes," she said, "I get so wrapped up in being a caretaker, I tend to lose some of the things I want to do."

Taking Care of Yourself

Sometimes, when I'm talking to a person who's too busy looking after others to take care of themselves, my spirit guides will give me the image of oxygen masks (like the ones they show you on planes during the preflight safety lecture).

When the flight attendant tells you to pull the mask over your face before dealing with your children, the point she's making is that if you're not in good shape, you're no use to those who are relying on you.

My spirit guides use it as a signal that this person needs to take better care of him or herself.

Since loyalty is one of the Caregiver type's greatest strengths, I asked her how it affected her.

Jan didn't even have to think. "I'm your best friend," she said, "I'll go to the wire for you. I'm very loyal, and I've fought a lot of battles for other people over the years."

"And how has preschool teaching been for you?"

"It's always felt really good. I've never felt I wanted to do anything else."

I've known Jan for five years and I can think of few people who are so suited for the job they're in. She's fortunate to have found her niche in the world. Equally fortunate are those who have been her students. Her influence on them will last a lifetime.

Most Caregivers are women because in most cultures women have a greater opportunity than men to embrace the advantage and nurture others. The risk that Caregivers run is that they'll neglect their own interests while putting others' needs ahead of their own. It's hard to avoid when the desire to nurture others comes from the soul and therefore feels so fulfilling.

The Educator Type

Advantage: Teaching

Risk: Verbosity

Many Educators are teachers and professors who are drawn to schools and places of learning where they can mix with other Educators. They tend to stick to subjects they know well, and use their natural aptitude for passing on information to get their message across to their students.

Since the advantage, teaching, is their focus, Educators are good communicators. The saying, "Those who can't, teach," is a slur against the Educator type, whose purpose is not to become an "expert," but to impart their wisdom, often learned over many lifetimes.

Brian is nearing the end of a four-year design course. In his parents' view, he has huge opportunities ahead of him. They want him to find an exciting job in a television company or working on movies. But is that also Brian's ambition?

Not at all. What Brian wants to do is teach. To him, it's a noble profession. To his parents, it's like settling for second best. To my spirit guides, it's totally consistent with his soul's plan for this lifetime.

Throughout our session, Brian did most of the talking, at one point borrowing my pen to draw a diagram to illustrate some point or other.

After a while I joked, "You really need to get yourself some students!"

Brian agreed. "Ever since I was a kid I've always wanted to teach. I used to watch my teachers and imagine I was them. I loved being in the classroom. I was the only student who didn't want to leave school."

The risk Educators run is verbosity, and they'll sometimes talk with no clear purpose. When they have a classroom to focus on (and it may not be a formal setup), they have an outlet for their love of communication. Without it, they may end up turning whoever's nearby into a student, which is exactly what happened in my office.

The Thinker Type

Advantage: Knowledge
Risk: Theory

Have you ever sat at a dinner table with someone who seems to be quietly sizing everyone up? That's either a Thinker or someone with a strong Thinker influence. Thinker types observe the world and learn from their analysis of it. As a result, they tend to be very much "in their heads."

One of the traits found in Thinkers is skepticism. They're rarely sold snake oil; they're far too cautious and would be careful to read the label first.

Often they analyze every last detail of something to the point where they can't make up their minds. They might spend more time planning their summer vacation than actually being there.

Thinker Restraint

Do you think of the classic academic as an emotional person who's given to dramatic, passionate outbursts? Probably not. The typical academic is a Thinker type, who feels more comfortable keeping his or her emotions within narrow limits.

Whenever someone sits down in my office and asks, "Can I take notes?" I can be almost certain they're a Thinker.

Most Thinkers are academically inclined. (The advantage is, after all, the accumulation of knowledge.) Kim, however, is a landscape gardener and because of a strong Performer influence, she doesn't look or act like a typical Thinker. Not only that, but she arrived in my office without a notebook. When my spirit guides told me she was a Thinker, I thought they might be wrong. Since a sure sign of a Thinker is a love of books, I asked her if she read much.

"Oh, yes," she said, "about 350 to 400 books a year!"

"That's more than one a day!" I said. "How on earth do you do it?"

"I don't sleep much," she joked. Then she thought about it and said, "I absorb them quickly. I look at whole sections, not single lines. I love opening a book and smelling and touching it," she said. "For me, reading is a very sensual experience."

Thinkers and Books

A love of reading is a characteristic most Thinkers share, yet every so often I'll meet one who's the exception to the rule. After two sessions in a week with Thinkers who didn't read, my spirit guides pointed out that "not every Thinker reads, but every Thinker thinks."

All Thinkers have to be careful not to substitute theory, the risk, for practice and become armchair experts. It's easy to be fooled into believing that reading about volcanoes is the same as seeing one for real.

The Creator Type

Advantage: Creativity
Risk: Distraction

Creator types have one foot on this plane and one in the next, which can give them a sense of not quite belonging to this world. They're often told they're not practical, like it's some kind of fault. In fact, it's just one of the qualities that makes them who they are.

Creators are found in abundance in art schools, dance academies, rock bands, and other places where they can surround themselves with creativity (the advantage). They make great engineers and builders, and often seek out professions where they can make things from scratch.

Creative Logic

Mathematician Andrew Wiles used his logical Thinker mind to figure out Fermat's last theorem: a problem that had baffled great minds for almost three hundred years. He had a secret power that helped him achieve this phenomenal feat: a Creator influence that gave him the ability to think visually.

A Creator influence also allows Thinkers to make huge leaps of imagination, and contributed to the success of such great scientists as Albert Einstein, Leo Szilard, Carl Sagan, and Richard Feynman.

James, an executive with a software company, came to me complaining that his career was no longer working for him. One of the first things my spirit guides revealed was that he's a Creator type, with a remarkable talent for drawing and painting as a result of having been a talented artist in a past life.

When I told him this, he said, "I love to draw. I try to draw something every day."

My guides added that he lacked confidence in himself, but others could see how good he was. He said, "Just yesterday, my wife told me that if she could draw like me, she'd be selling her work in galleries."

The sense of smell helps connect many people, particularly highly sensitive Creator types, to past lives. It's one of the reasons the smell of spices or flowers can trigger an emotional response. My spirit guides told me James painted in oils, which gave him a comforting connection with his past life as a painter. The moment I told him it was the smell, as much as anything else, that drew him to that particular medium, he said, "Absolutely! That's so right."

James is being guided to devote more time to his art in this lifetime. Creativity, according to my guides, is something his soul is "crying out for." And if he can find a job that offers more opportunity to express his creativity, he's going to be a lot happier in the future.

Many athletes and dancers are Creator types who use their bodies to express who they are. Sometimes mathematicians and scientists will choose—prior to incarnation—a Creator influence to help connect them to the Soul World and the inspiration it offers.

Creator Idealism

Idealism is often regarded as a failing, but the Creator uses this trait to observe a need or a potential, and works to fill the gap. Creators are visionaries and artists who excel at seeing the big picture. For that reason, they usually avoid getting caught up in minutiae, which they find boring.

The words Creators hear most as they're growing up are: "You're too sensitive." If parents and teachers could only say, "You're highly sensitive, and that's great," creators would end up with a lot more confidence than they so often do.

The risk associated with these highly imaginative souls is that they're easily distracted. Older-soul Creators will wander about in mismatched socks or with the price label still attached to their jacket. The stereotypical absent-minded professor is a Creator (or sometimes a Thinker with a Creator influence). A little preoccupation is fine (creative people have to dream), but it's important to check in with the Physical Plane from time to time.

The Performer Type
Advantage: Communication
Risk: Pretension

A caricature of the Performer type can be seen in people like Jim Carrey, Bette Midler, Eddie Murphy, and Robin Williams. It's hard to imagine what any of them would do without an audience.

Performers are comfortable being in the spotlight, and they often go out of their way to get the attention they crave. One of my Performer clients told me that when she was seven years old, she stepped up on a chair, held out her arms, and declared, "I'm going to be the greatest actress the world has ever known!"

If you have a Performer child who won't do what they're asked, try turning it into a game. Performers are playful, and always far more motivated to do things if they're fun.

More than any other soul type, they need applause, both literally and in the form of hugs and demonstrative words of appreciation. They're often generous with their praise, in the hope that it will be reciprocated.

If you've ever been backstage after a play, you'll know what I mean. It's there, too, that you might have witnessed individuals who display the risk: pretentiousness, or acting a part instead of being themselves.

In this young-soul world, Performers, like Creators, are under-valued. We may think the public has a fascination with them, given how many of them make the covers of supermarket tabloids, but what we're seeing is more a young-soul obsession with celebrity.

In reality, Performers have a lot of difficulty making a living in their traditional roles as communicators and entertainers, so they often have to bring their talents to other arenas. Being a trial lawyer, for example, is a terrific career for someone who needs an audience. Yet Performers turn up pretty much everywhere.

Cheryl works for a major bookseller. During our session, when I discovered she was a Performer type, I said, "You should have been an actress."

She burst into tears and wailed, "It's all I ever wanted!"

The problem was that her parents discouraged it. They felt she was setting herself up for disappointment by even thinking of such a precarious career.

With my spirit guides' encouragement, Cheryl has begun taking acting classes while she continues in the job for which she's well suited, thanks to her strong Thinker influence.

The Christmas Present

During our session, my spirit guides asked Cheryl what she wanted for Christmas. She laughed and said, "My girlfriends and I were asking each other that question the other night. I told them I wanted a boyfriend."

My spirit guides assured her that her wish would come true. It was early February when I received an email from Cheryl telling me she'd met someone at the office Christmas party, and they hadn't been apart since.

Performer types sometimes forget they're not on stage. You might share an intimate secret with them, and they'll repeat it at full volume just to ensure a wider audience.

Performers are passionate people who are generally more open with their emotions than other types. Communication, the advantage, is fundamentally important to them. If you have a Performer child, you can drive them nuts if you don't pay attention when they're trying to tell you something.

The Hunter Type

Advantage: Activity
Risk: Inflexibility

They say a Mountie always gets his man. If he's a Hunter type, whose determination is one of his strongest traits, it's not at all surprising. This soul type is active, task-oriented, and immensely practical.

When a woman is a Hunter type—or has that influence—she'll have an aggressive edge that will help her thrive in a male-dominated world.

Elaine is a Level 10 soul who worked until recently in the gritty world of law and order as a public defender. Her soul type is that of a Thinker, and, as with a lot of Thinkers, when I asked her a question there would be a momentary delay as she processed the information and decided on her response.

She's analytical, gentle, and humorous, yet under her unassuming exterior lurks a secret weapon: a very strong Hunter influence.

When I saw she had this, I said, "You're tougher than you look! I bet when you get your teeth into something you don't let go. You must have intimidated the prosecutors you went up against."

Elaine grinned. "They called me the Bulldog," she said. "In the municipal court, I went months without being defeated. I always argued with integrity. I felt a huge responsibility to my clients.

"I could identify with most of them. Prosecutors would joke that I loved my clients. You know, I really think that was true. I had more respect for my clients than I had for most judges and prosecutors."

Thanks to her Hunter influence and old-soul sensibilities, Elaine is a tenacious champion of the underdog. Though now retired, her social consciousness is leading her to Georgia next where, like the Hennessey sisters, she plans to protest the teaching of torture at the School of the Americas.

Hunters are comfortable working both individually and in teams, and are drawn to sports like football. On the field, they can join with other Hunters and enjoy the thrill of the chase in a game with clear rules and objectives. Hunters are highly competitive and like to win.

They'll work hard to put food on their family's table, as they did fifty thousand years ago when the survival of the tribe depended on their skills. Back then, discipline and loyalty were essential for those whose success, and even survival, depended on their comrades. Modern Hunters still carry this trait.

Being so goal-oriented, all Hunter types run the risk of being inflexible: "I've done it like this all my life—I'm not going to change now."

The advantage for Hunters is activity. In a movie, we can all instinctively relate to the Hunter-type cop when his boss yells, "You're off the case!" and gives him a desk job.

The Leader Type

Advantage: Authority
Risk: Intransigence

Leader types are relatively rare. A little goes a long way, however. They tend to choose tall bodies as part of their life plan. This helps them to stand out from the crowd, even though their natural charisma and air of authority (the advantage) will tend to do that, regardless of what they look like.

When Leader types are children, they often show a marker, a sign of things to come. They'll surround themselves with a court of their friends. Their peers will clearly see them as leaders, not followers, and that's something that will continue throughout adulthood.

Leaders are not used to taking instructions from others, or being in anything but a position of authority. Not surprisingly, the risk most often seen in them is intransigence: the inability to take others' advice.

Many Leader parents also have Leader children. The reason for this is so that Mom or Dad can model appropriate ways to use the power—something they'll do with varying degrees of success.

One evening in 1975, Michael's father sat him down and told him he was leaving for good. "As he spoke, time seemed to slow down and I had a kind of out-of-body experience," Michael said. "I knew my life was changing in a very big way."

That night, eleven-year-old Michael looked in the mirror and said, "That's it. Your childhood is over."

From that point on, he was thrown into the role of leader— just like his father, and his father before him.

Leaders in the World

Younger-soul Leaders are more frequently drawn to the corporate world. (Since Leaders often choose tall bodies, it's one of the reasons CEOs are often taller than average.) As their souls age, Leaders no longer have the same need to exert their power quite so overtly.

"What happened to me was exactly what happened to Dad," Michael said. "Grandpa was severely alcoholic, and left the family. Dad was pushed into a leadership role at age eight. He had to take care of a sickly brother and a younger sister.

"I had my mom and two sisters to look after. My mom was in shambles. I knew they were relying on me and I couldn't let them down," he said.

Like many Leader types, Michael is well over six feet tall. And like many Leaders, he had a Leader father to follow. Jack, his dad, was an AFL champion quarterback and stood six feet four inches.

Michael also excelled at sports. "I believe what got me through it all was basketball and church," he said. But there was something else: "Sometime after Dad left, I remember hearing a voice telling me to stay the course. I don't know why, but I trusted that through thick and thin—and there was a lot more thin than thick. We faced some huge challenges."

Things between Michael and his dad have changed a lot over the years. "I never felt resentful. I knew if I did, I'd never get beyond that. Now Dad's dying of cancer, and I see how his childhood affected him. I visited him recently and we got to talk about stuff. He's got a lot of regrets about the past, and particularly about the opportunities he lost because he couldn't trust anyone. I said, 'Dad, you always had to be in command. It was way too much responsibility on a little boy's shoulders.' He just gripped my hand and wept."

Many Leaders find it impossible to be subservient to anyone. (Imagine Sean Connery or Elvis flipping burgers at McDonald's.) I asked Michael what it's like for him being a Leader type in the workplace.

"Power comes from everyone getting together for a common goal," he said. "I enjoy collaborating, but once we clap hands and come out of the huddle—let me run!"

When Michael said that, it was clearer than ever that the apple didn't fall very far from the tree.

The Spiritualist Type
Advantage: Improvement
Risk: Obsession

My Spiritualist type clients are some of the most compassionate people you could meet. They tend to have an air of otherworldliness about them. Like Creator types, they find themselves with one foot in this world and one in the Soul World.

As younger souls, they're drawn to the priesthood, but once they get to be old souls, they become less religious and more spiritual. The problem then becomes finding an outlet for their spirituality.

The advantage associated with Spiritualist types is improvement. They want to help others fulfill their potential and, though they don't consciously know it, complete their life plans. And that's why they can make a huge impact on others—even after they're gone.

When Lois, an elderly Spiritualist type, died, the family invited me to the funeral, followed by a reception at the care center where she'd spent her last years.

Not only was Lois a Spiritualist type, but so was her daughter-in-law, Sheila, and her four-year-old granddaughter, Lucy. All three generations had one thing in common: a strong connection to the Soul World. Lucy, particularly, is highly psychic.

It wasn't until Lucy saw the empty room at the care center that she finally realized Grandma wasn't coming home. She broke down, sobbing uncontrollably.

Then, a few days later, I got a call from her mother, who wanted to tell me what happened when they got home.

Lucy was still very upset at bedtime, so she slept with Mom and Dad. In the early hours of the morning, Sheila was awakened by what she thought was a voice in the room. As her eyes grew accustomed to the dark, she could see that Lucy was still lying in bed beside her. The room was silent for a minute, and Sheila began to think she'd been mistaken. Then, suddenly, Lucy spoke. "I think I understand," she said. Sheila hardly recognized her daughter's voice. It sounded grown-up, and quite "matter-of-fact."

Sheila slowly became aware of her mother-in-law's presence in the room. "It was like a shadow," she told me, "but I could see exactly where she was standing at the side of the bed."

Sheila knew Lois was communicating with her too, but she didn't seem to be using words. Sheila can only express whatever message she got as "Love-love-love-love-love . . . "

Lucy, however, was obviously hearing and understanding much more. She spoke with Grandma for several minutes. From Lucy's responses, Sheila could tell Grandma was explaining why she had to leave her body, but how she'd still always be there in spirit. Lucy ended her part of the conversation with these words: "Oh, now I see . . . you had to go home."

"Then Lois started to rise up and over the bed," Sheila said. "I looked at Lucy and saw that her eyes were open and they were following her as she floated over us and left through the door."

The next day, Lucy was brighter. Whatever had passed between her and Grandma had left her in a happier frame of mind. Grandma had returned to reassure the fellow Spiritualists in the family that she was still with them.

Spiritualist Values

Spiritualist types want to make the world a better place and bring healing to humanity. As a result, they'll often apply their compassion and inspirational qualities to seemingly unrelated areas of life.

John Lennon, for example, expressed himself through his music. The lyrics to "Imagine" are the heartfelt sentiments of an old-soul Spiritualist.

The risk seen most often in Spiritualists is that they may slip from wanting to change people for the better into becoming obsessive. Like the proverbial Boy Scout, they may help you across the road— even if you don't want to go.

The Transformer Type
Advantage: Unity
Risk: Unworldliness

Transformer types are very few and far between. Though you're unlikely to actually meet a Transformer in your lifetime, their influence can reach you over great distances.

They're always Level 10 souls, and are a combination of Spiritualist and Leader types. As a result, they have charisma, compassion wisdom, and the ability to lead and inspire. The awareness that all of us are connected is at its strongest in Transformers.

Transformers always manage to transcend the Illusion. That's one reason why they're never materialistic.

Their purpose is to incite change. They bring their unique qualities to earth at times when our consciousness needs raising a notch. In fact, one sign of Transformers is that they and their followers (they always develop a following) create huge social, political, or spiritual shifts.

Since Transformers have Spiritualist traits, they tend to express themselves in spiritual terms. And being old souls, their message is always one of peace, unity (the advantage), love, and equality.

Transformers and Younger Souls

Transformers threaten the status quo. And that's not something young-soul politicians and leaders want to encourage. That's why it's not unusual to hear of Transformers being imprisoned or assassinated. Martin Luther King Jr. and Mohandas Gandhi were both imprisoned and killed.

Every Transformer throughout history has been highly inspirational. Even those whose soul age and type come close to making them Transformers can inspire others in profound ways. Nelson Mandela and John Lennon, both Level 10 Spiritualists with Leader influences (not true Transformers) have left lasting impressions on the world.

The risk associated with Transformers is a disregard for their own safety. They turn down the offer of bodyguards or leave safe areas and put themselves at risk. Being such old souls means they have no fear of death.

· · ·

As you can see, each soul type has its strengths and weaknesses. If your house goes up in flames, you're going to want a bunch of burly Hunter types to come to the rescue. And if you need a good accountant, you might be best off with a Thinker or someone with that influence.

In this society, certain personality traits are more appreciated than others. We overvalue stoicism and practicality, and undervalue sensitivity and spirituality. Yet every trait has its purpose. If everyone was stoic and practical, where would we find our artists and poets?

If someone puts you down because you can't do something they can, remember that you have abilities they don't. The important thing is to recognize your natural strengths and weaknesses.

So, next, let's determine who you are, and what particular qualities you brought into the world.

Discover Your Soul Type

Begin by entering a meditative state (see page 14), and calling in your spirit guides. Ask them for their help in determining your soul type. Use the list below to remind you of the focus and trails associated with each type. As before, use your intuition. Remember, the purpose of this exercise, and the reason spirit guides play such an important part in it, is to find out who you really are, not just who you've always assumed you are.

Soul Type	Focus	Traits
Helper	Service	Dedication, Stoicism
Caregiver	Nurturing	Empathy, Loyalty
Educator	Teaching	Erudition, Eloquence

Soul Type	Focus	Traits
Thinker	Knowledge	Restraint, Rationality
Creator	Creativity	Sensitivity, Idealism
Performer	Communication	Passion, Playfulness
Hunter	Activity	Determination, Practicality
Leader	Authority	Charisma, Wisdom
Spiritualist	Improvement	Compassion, Spirituality
Transformer	Unity	Inspiration, Love

Soul Type:_____

Now, go through the list once more, looking first for the focus that has the second strongest resonance with you. The soul type associated with that focus is your primary influence.

Primary Influence:_____

Now do the same for the traits that have the third strongest resonance with you. The soul type associated with those traits will be your secondary influence.

Secondary Influence:_____

Ask your spirit guides to support you in manifesting your soul type. Repeat the following:

"I call upon my spirit guides, acting in my highest interest, to help me manifest my soul type and allow me to live the life my soul intended."

When you've finished, thank your spirit guides, and tell them, "Session over."

If you have difficulty deciding on your soul type, you may find it helpful to ask yourself what you wanted to be as a child, what you want to do in the future, and what's missing in your life now. Try to look beyond simply what you do to make a living. And if you're still having problems after doing that, ask yourself if the advantage or risk associated with a particular soul type resonates with you.

• • •

Popeye was given to proudly declaring, "I yam what I yam," and it's my hope that you'll learn to do the same.

Understanding your soul type will help you develop true self-acceptance. So, when someone criticizes you for simply being yourself, you can turn around and tell them, "That's just the way I am," not as an excuse, but as a self-assured statement of your individuality.

At this point you should have a clear idea of who you are. But does that explain what you're doing here? That will be answered in the next chapter when we look at your soul's Missions. Understanding that is the key to discovering your life's purpose.

4: THE DOOR TO ACHIEVEMENT
Missions: Your Life's Purpose

Missions are the soul's way of giving each lifetime a focus. The purpose of any life can be discovered by investigating its missions.
—THE AUTHOR'S CAUSAL GUIDES

What is your purpose? The answer is simple: you're here to live the life your soul intended. The secret, of course, is figuring out just exactly what it is your soul wants.

As you step through the Door to Achievement, you'll discover that every one of us is on a mission. In fact, we're on more than one. We all have a primary mission, and one or two secondary missions. This ensures that every single life, no matter how mundane, has a purpose.

So, where do these missions come from?

Again, they're part of your life plan. Before you were born, your soul reviewed lessons learned and those still to be learned, and chose specific goals for this lifetime. Your missions are the "big lessons" it hopes to learn this time around.

Your missions are with you from the day you're born. During that time, they'll affect everything you do. Ken, whose primary mission—Exploration—we'll explore later in the chapter, told me that when he was four his mother found him in the neighboring stockyard at the top of a five-story ladder. "I could have died a thousand times," he said of his childhood. Without that particular mission, he'd never have taken such extreme risks.

By selecting different missions for each lifetime, your soul ensures that you get a well-rounded education. If you were planning to be an academic, you might choose a mission of Examination. If your soul saw the possibility of you running your own company, it might have selected a mission of Control.

Most of the planet was dragged into World War II by a Level 5 soul on a mission of Change. Like many messianic leaders, Adolf Hitler was a Spiritualist type (remember the risk of obsession?), and like almost everyone with this mission, he was driven to make the world a different place. (It probably goes without saying that he was completely caught up in the Illusion.)

His soul type imbued him with the ability to inspire. The mission of Control gave him the desire to remake the world according to his vision of how it should be. Together they created a monster.

Yet this combination is anything but rare. Many people have this soul type and mission, and don't end up causing the death of millions. That's because missions can be used for both selfish and altruistic reasons.

Hitler had a soul, just like everyone else, and no soul ever wants to take another human life. But Hitler, being so blinded by the Illusion, ignored his soul's guidance. He could have used his power to make the world a better place. Instead, he chose to act from a place of aggression and self-interest.

You choose your missions for one simple reason: experience. That's what motivates your soul. Missions are its way of achieving its goals.

The Ten Missions

- The mission of Change
- The mission of Exploration
- The mission of Examination
- The mission of Flow
- The mission of Control
- The mission of Connection
- The mission of Reliance
- The mission of Healing
- The mission of Avoidance
- The mission of Love

As you read through the descriptions of the ten missions, don't just look to find yourself, but see if you can identify your family and friends, too. By figuring out everyone else's missions, you'll see where you are in relation to them—and that will help you better understand yourself. (Everything, as they say, is relative.)

Though we may each appear to be following many different paths at once, each of us has just one primary and one or two secondary missions. Your primary mission tends to be more outwardly focused and permanent, and your secondary mission, which is also one of the ten, tends to be more internal and may "float."

The Mission of Change
Advantage: Improvement
Risk: Novelty

Change is one of the most outwardly focused missions. People with this mission can make indelible marks on the world. But it also has a strong internal aspect. It creates the need for continual forward movement. And it encourages you to look for ways to correct flaws, real or imagined. If you have a shelf full of self-help books, it's a good indication that Change is your mission.

Eleanor is a Thinker type who sat down for our session and, quite typically, pulled out a notebook. What was not quite so "Thinkerly" was her body language. Some of my Thinker clients display their emotions with a level of abandonment most often associated with cigar-store Indians. Eleanor, however, expressed herself using superlatives accompanied by appropriate hand gestures.

What I was seeing was a Thinker type with a very strong Creator influence—a combination often found in those, like Albert Einstein, who combine linear thinking with the ability to make huge leaps of imagination.

I could tell immediately that she was a mathematician. And, seeing she had a mission of Change, I said, "I bet you want to leave the world a better place."

Eleanor stopped writing. "I really do!" she said. "I think about it all the time."

Being an older soul, and also having a Spiritualist influence, Eleanor is drawn to helping others. "In third grade I began tutoring other kids in math—I was done with my own work so quickly," she said.

"So you chose a career in math pretty early?" I asked.

"Math chose me," she said, "not vice-versa."

Eleanor's mission of Change has helped her spot a gap in the market for math primers. She plans to change the world by introducing a more creative and interesting way to teach math to children.

Since Eleanor's mission also has an internal aspect to it, I said, "I expect you've bought quite a few self-help books in your time."

She just laughed and said, "Oh yes."

The advantage, improvement, is designed to prevent complacency. No matter what you achieve, you'll never rest on your laurels for very long before the need for change will have you moving forward again.

Regardless of your soul type, if you're on this mission you'll run into a risk. It's a thirst for novelty, or the "thrill of the new." Whether it's a business or a relationship, you might neglect the old in favor of what seems fresher or more interesting.

The Mission of Exploration

Advantage: Empiricism
Risk: Dissipation

A mission of Exploration is chosen to give your soul the maximum opportunity for having real-world experiences. In fact, some younger souls with this mission literally become explorers. The advantage is empiricism: learning about the world for yourself.

Regardless of the age of your soul, if this is your mission, life will never be dull. If you're looking for tranquility, you may have to wait until next time.

On the downside, the risk, dissipation, means that without a clear focus you can end up seeking out new experiences without considering whether or not they're useful to you. You often see it in the person who wants to do so many things that their energy becomes dissipated or watered down.

The Danger of Dissipation

As a guitar-obsessed high-school student with a mission of Exploration, Jonas won the prestigious Louis Armstrong Jazz Award, while also becoming an expert in martial arts, boxing, and baseball, and taking the number two spot in the state for wrestling.

In college, he won more major awards for his virtuoso soloing and played in orchestras, jazz bands, and musicals, and did a stint with the Tommy Dorsey band.

He's been a session musician, a roofer, a composer, an arranger, a groundskeeper, a carpenter, a guitar teacher, a pool cleaner, and has even built laser/hologram machines.

And that's the problem.

Like many people with a mission of Exploration, Jonas (a Level 10 Creator) has encountered the risk: dissipation. He's meant to be a musician. It's what his soul planned for him in this life. However, spreading himself too thinly has prevented him from fully capitalizing on his amazing talent.

With my Causal guides' support, he's working on becoming fully engaged in his life plan, which is to be a musician and performer.

Not many of my clients with a mission of Exploration still live where they were born. That's because travel, even at an early age, is an urge few of them can resist.

Ken came to me with what he described as "hundreds of questions." His biggest, however, was what to do with his retirement—something that was looming large on the horizon.

When I saw Ken had a mission of Exploration, I knew he wasn't ready for a life of leisure. Then my spirit guides showed me Ken sitting in a pavement café in Siena, Italy.

"You're going to travel," I said, and I told him what I saw.

Ken was excited. It turned out this was exactly what he wanted to do—though he had to admit he was meeting some resistance. Only a few days before, a friend of his had raised all sorts of obstacles, such as what would happen if he got sick or even died while in another country.

"From what I can see, you're far more likely to die climbing the *campanile* in Venice than in bed in the United States," I said.

Ken smiled and leaned forward. "Then, as I told my friend, I'll die happy," he said.

My spirit guides gave these parting words: "Be happy, don't worry, renew your passport."

Ken laughed out loud. "They're right," he said, "My passport *has* expired!"

When I last spoke to him, Ken was completing arrangements for a six-month trip through Central America.

Early Signs of a Mission of Exploration

One of the first things my daughter learned to say was, "My do it by my own." Like any child with a mission of Exploration, she wants to figure out things for herself.

On a transatlantic flight to the UK, I could see my little six-year-old Thinker type was struggling with the remote control for her video screen. I leaned over and tried to point out that she had it stuck on game mode. Quite typically, she held the remote as far away as possible from me and told me she had the situation well under control.

I pulled one side of her headphones away from her ear and said, "Sweetheart, why is it you never do a thing I tell you?"

In typical Thinker fashion, she thought for a second or two then said, quite unaware of the rhetorical nature of my question, "Because I can usually think of a better way to do it myself."

The Mission of Examination

Advantage: Understanding

Risk: Indecision

Socrates said, "The unexamined life is not worth living." This might be the motto of those whose mission is Examination.

Focused inwardly, it will inspire you to investigate your thoughts and actions to give your life meaning. Focused outwardly, it will give you a thirst for knowledge and a desire to make sense of the world. The advantage is understanding, which is why Examination is a popular mission with writers, academics, philosophers, and scientists.

Your soul type will affect how you express this, or any other mission. A Thinker type will examine the world intellectually; a Spiritualist type will come at it from a more emotional angle. A Creator type might choose to examine art, perhaps as an historian.

One side effect of this mission is that you may accumulate knowledge regardless of its use. The risk associated with Examination is what one of my clients termed analysis-paralysis: where options are weighed up to the point where no decision is made.

Lynn's life has been dissected, examined, reexamined, and reassembled. She's a typical Thinker on a mission of Examination. She continually analyzes herself and every aspect of her world. And when it comes to making decisions, she gets so wrapped up in the pros and cons she finds she can't take action.

Toward the end of the session, she asked for help with a letter she was writing to her lawyer. She read it to me.

"It sounds fine," I said. "What's the problem?"

She thought the second paragraph sounded a little aggressive. I told her that perhaps it did, so she changed a few words and felt better about it.

Two days later, I got a call. She wanted to reread the letter to me. It hadn't changed much since we'd last spoken. I suggested she should send it as it was. Unfortunately, by this time, the risk, indecision, had set in.

That weekend I got yet another call. Now she was convinced the wording was too casual. At this point, I should mention that the letter was not about a huge custody case or some other life-and-death matter. It was about her lawyer overcharging her fifty dollars or so on a bill from months before.

"Perhaps you should just send it?" I suggested.

She agreed.

The next time I spoke to Lynn, I asked her about the letter. She said she'd decided just to drop the whole matter.

The Mission of Flow

Advantage: Acceptance
Risk: Inertia

A mission of Flow lets you move smoothly through life. The purpose of its advantage, acceptance, is to help you learn to take life as it comes. Doors will open and opportunities will present themselves without great effort on your part. The secret is to recognize the opportunities when they come along.

This mission is almost always chosen to compensate for several consecutive lifetimes of struggle and hardship.

One of my clients, a recently retired scientist with a mission of Flow, conceded that she's lived a "charmed life." She sailed through school and college, was offered a job before she'd even finished her training, won promotion when she needed it, and never had any problems finding funding for projects she worked on. She felt that help from others had always been available.

There is an old story that you've probably heard before, but it illustrates the risk associated with this mission.

It's about a man who gets caught up in a flood and climbs onto the roof of his house for safety. As the waters rise, he prays to God who promises to save him.

Soon, a rescue team in a boat arrives. "Jump in!" they shout.

The man refuses to get on board saying, "No thanks, God will save me."

An hour later, as the waters threaten to engulf him, a helicopter hovers overhead and drops a rope. Once again, he refuses the offer of help. "No thanks, God will save me," he shouts.

Minutes later, he drowns.

The next thing he knows, he's standing at the Pearly Gates. He sees God and says, "What happened? I thought you were going to save me."

And God replies, "I sent you a boat, I sent you a helicopter . . . "

The risk for anyone with this mission is inertia. They may fail to recognize opportunities when they present themselves, or let them pass by rather than taking action.

Children with a mission of Flow are often the ones we describe as easygoing or even passive. But what about those who are less open to submitting to the will of others?

The Mission of Control

Advantage: Authority

Risk: Intransigence

When a mission of Control is focused internally, it gives people the need to have a huge say in their destiny. They won't want others making decisions on their behalf, or telling them what to do.

And when it's focused outwardly, they have the need to run

things. Being in charge comes from their soul, and gives them a natural air of authority. When they tell you something, you get the sense it's coming from someone who knows what they're talking about.

In some ways, they can appear like Leader types. The only thing that gives them away is their absence of the Leader's characteristic charisma.

Laurel's fifteen-year-old daughter, Kerry, has a mission of Control. I asked Laurel what raising a child like her had been like.

"Right from the beginning, she's never taken no for an answer. When she was small, I had to sleep with her every night for a whole year. If I didn't, she'd scream the house down.

"Sometimes if I won't let her have her way, she'll fly into a rage and get violent. One time, we had to stop her from throwing a brick through the car window."

Running the Show

A person with a mission of Control differs from a Leader type in that theirs is a way of acting rather than a way of being. Having this mission allows all soul types the opportunity to take on positions of authority.

A Performer type with this mission will be every bit as good at running things as a Leader type. They'll simply do it a little more flamboyantly.

Laurel is a Level 10 Creator type. As such, her "path of least resistance" approach causes her to concede arguments just to keep the peace. "For Kerry, it's really important to be right. Even when I know I'm right, I'll sometimes let things slide because I simply can't convince her she's wrong."

Raising a child with this mission is always hard. Control may have been chosen by Kerry's soul to help her run a corporation when she's in her forties. However, getting to that point may be tough.

The mission of Control can be hard on Kerry, too. "She's afraid to show any kind of vulnerability," Laurel said. "She has to have A grades all the time. There is no pressure from me. I've told her it's okay to get a B."

Like a lot of people with this mission, Kerry likes routine. Controlling her environment is as important as controlling herself and those around her.

"She hates it when we change our car, and she got very upset when we didn't take our regular annual trip to California," Laurel said. "Kerry's a pack rat. She still has the same little snuggle toy from when she was born. It looks like a threadbare blob, but she can't let go of anything."

There is one serious risk. In both children and adults, a mission of Control can lead to intransigence: a refusal to take the advice of others, or to consider changing a decision once it's been made.

Some wit once said he felt honored to know his teenage son while he still knew everything. His son might well have been on this mission.

The Mission of Connection
Advantage: Intimacy
Risk: Identification

Touch is vitally important to human beings. The reason is that close physical contact allows intimacy (the advantage of the mission of Connection) between souls. It's why babies need hugs, why massage is good for us, and one of the major reasons why, according to the Mayo Clinic, married couples live longer and are healthier and happier than singles.

For those with a mission of Connection, touch is as essential to their survival as oxygen. Without it, they can literally wither and die. From babies in orphanages to prisoners in solitary confinement, the people who will suffer most are the ones with this mission.

And here's a statistic that may surprise you: over 80 percent of us have Connection as our primary mission.

It's why so many of us need the company of others. Human beings are not meant to be alone. Without a mission of Connection, a person may be reasonably comfortable without a partner. But the majority of us are meant to be in intimate relationships, and we'll suffer a kind of separation anxiety when we're denied the comfort that comes from having another soul with whom we can share our lives.

Multiple Missions

Connection, being so common, actually transcends missions, but is considered one of the ten when it comes to describing a person's purpose.

Someone with a mission of Connection will always have two secondary missions. Those who fall into the 20 percent who don't have Connection as their primary mission will have only one.

Connection pushes you out into the world to make contact with people on a soul level. It will give you a natural ability to relate to others, and a desire for unity and harmony.

Nadia's social calendar is full to the point where she can't meet all the demands made on her.

"I've got people around me all the time, so why am I so lonely?" she asked me.

I said, "Because of your mission of Connection, your soul is crying out for intimacy. It wants close one-on-one contact with other souls. You've got genuine friends, but you're too busy to nurture your relationships with them. And they feel undervalued because you have so little time for them."

Nadia could see the problem immediately. "My last boyfriend left because he was fed up with having to make appointments to see me," she said.

Much of the conflict in her life comes from a past-life-related fear of loneliness. To counter the fear, she surrounds herself with people.

Yet what she really needs to both overcome the fear and complete her mission is deeper friendships. Her soul is going to be a lot happier having a candlelit dinner for two, where intimacy can be reached, than making small talk in a crowded room.

Certain people with a mission of Connection, especially the more outgoing types like Performers, want to make sure those around them are connecting, too. If they see someone standing alone at a party, they'll take it upon themselves to strike up a conversation or introduce them to someone else.

While we spoke, Nadia displayed the most common risk associated with this mission: overidentifying with other people's suffering. As she told me about a friend's struggles with the immigration authorities, tears trickled down her cheeks.

It's important to remember that there is a difference between expressing empathy and feeling someone else's pain to the point where it affects you as much or even more than it does them.

The Mission of Avoidance

Advantage: Tranquility

Risk: Isolation

In total contrast to the mission of Connection is the mission of Avoidance. Alexandra is someone whose soul chose this after several very dramatic lifetimes. To put it simply, her soul needed a rest.

Like many people with a mission of Avoidance, Alexandra has a natural air of sophistication. Sitting in my office wearing a simple blouse and pants, she exuded the kind of elegance that wouldn't seem out of place on the boulevards of Paris.

I'd met her a number of times before, but on this occasion she looked completely worn out. Several years before, she'd taken over a café. To begin with, she was excited and inspired, but after she split up with her husband, and he withdrew his support, the long hours and stresses of working seven days a week began to catch up with her. The initial enthusiasm had long ago worn off. Now all she wanted to do was sell the business and go traveling.

"You'll find a buyer—a woman—but it may take some time," I told her.

Alexandra looked deflated. "It's gotten to the point where I really can't face being behind the counter anymore."

I wasn't in the least surprised. With a mission of Avoidance, she was never meant to be out in the world this much. She agreed wholeheartedly.

I asked her if she'd always recognized her soul's need for tranquility.

"Oh, yes," she said. "After I left college, I traveled to Europe. I lasted a couple of months in London before I became overwhelmed by all the people and the noise. I escaped to a cabin by a lake in Norway. That was when I realized just how much I needed tranquility.

"For years after that, I'd go to a cabin on my own every six weeks. Sometimes I'd just pull down the shades and sleep for two or three days. And every time I came back, I'd be totally restored. I'd have to do it. If I didn't, I'd get sick."

It took Alexandra a long eighteen months to find a buyer (a woman), and when she told me the news she was like a different person. It would be another few weeks until the deal was completed, but her mind was firmly fixed on the future.

"What do you plan to do now," I asked.

"Next stop is a hammock in Hawaii!" she said. "I plan to sleep for a week."

Tranquility is the advantage in the case of a mission of Avoidance. Without it, someone like Alexandra can suffer terribly from continual overstimulation. The risk is that of isolation. When I told Alexandra that, she admitted there had been times when she'd felt like retreating to her cabin in the woods and never coming out again.

The Mission of Healing

Advantage: Recovery
Risk: Obligation

Healing is a common mission for those in the medical, caring, or teaching professions. Mother Teresa, a Level 10 Hunter type, had this mission, as did Florence Nightingale, a Level 6 Helper.

The goal of this mission is to learn about healing in the broadest sense. Outwardly, it's achieved by making others better. Inwardly, it's about healing trauma from this lifetime and ones in the past. The advantage is recovery: helping to return yourself or others to a normal or improved state.

In this lifetime, Anne, a Level 9 Spiritualist type, has chosen, as she has many times before, a mission of Healing.

I asked her if she'd always known her mission. "I knew in second grade that I wanted to be a doctor," she said. "But it wasn't until I had a seeing-the-light experience that I knew for sure. I was sixteen, and I was in the choir at midnight mass. I saw a warm, creamy white light come streaming through the stained-glass window. I don't know how long it lasted, but I felt a message that my purpose was to heal, and when the light was gone, I had total clarity about my future."

Yet it was only after author and psychic Judith Orloff described her as a "healer" that she began to see her purpose as broader than just being a doctor.

"I spoke to her after a lecture she gave," Anne said. "I praised her for her writing, and said how important I thought it was for people to learn the importance of spirituality in medicine. She signed my copy of her book, but it wasn't until I got home that I saw she'd written: 'To Anne—a healer. Love, Judy.'

"The idea of being a healer scared me. I was trained as a scientifically minded surgeon, but that one word helped me face my own reality. It was a wake-up call. I realized I had to accept who I was. To own it; to use it."

Anne's empathy has always been one of her strongest talents. She describes her secret as, "Touch, talk, and listen." As her career developed, she found that she had a way with cancer patients and those who were dying. "I've helped many patients, even babies, cross over. One of my elderly patients wouldn't die until I was with her."

Like many people with a mission of Healing, Anne has had to learn to deal with the risk, which is obligation, that causes many healers to feel they have a duty to help others. A few years ago, with my spirit guides' encouragement, she cut back from a grueling six-day week to one that allows her more time to relax. Now she meditates twice a day, and does two to three hours every Sunday morning.

When I asked Anne if being in such a high-pressure career was an effort for her, she said, "I can't not do it."

And I believe that's right. Anne is on a mission of Healing, and it would be impossible to imagine her doing anything else.

The Mission of Reliance
Advantage: Dependence
Risk: Obduracy

Simon is eleven years old. He was recently rushed to the hospital, where he lay unconscious in the intensive care unit for several days. The reason: a severe allergic reaction from a single bite of a cheese sandwich.

Simon was born with brain-bleed and his right temporal lobe missing. He's also virtually blind, though his difficulty in communicating makes testing impossible. In his first few years of life, he had as many as forty seizures a day.

He was given a series of heavy-duty medications, which put a temporary stop to the seizures until, pretty soon, they began to lose their effect. His mother, Jennifer, told me what eventually happened.

"The medication robbed him of his personality. It made him really vicious, and on top of that, he'd be vomiting all the time," she said. "And then he started having night terrors.

"One night he woke up screaming, and was literally climbing the wall. It was terrifying. He was like a wild animal. I had to peel his fingernails from the wall to get him down. At that point I was going crazy. I had a new baby and was totally sleep-deprived.

"I thought that if it kept up I'd strangle him. He was so disruptive, demanding, and miserable. Then I met someone who told me about food allergies, and how a change in diet had stopped the seizures in her son."

Jennifer spent the next few weeks weaning Simon off his medications and experimenting with various foods. Within a month, the seizures and night terrors had stopped.

"I finally got the real Simon back," Jennifer said. "Once he was off the medications and avoiding dairy and wheat, he was a different child."

Then came the incident that ended up with Simon having convulsions when someone left a cheese sandwich within his reach. He was released from hospital a few days later, and Jennifer was pleased that for the first time no one had suggested putting him back on medication. "They don't even try any more," she said. "I'm informed and insistent. He used to be a zombie, but without the meds he's finally learning to speak."

Jennifer reminded me of something my spirit guides told her several years ago when we first spoke. They said that she and Simon had an agreement on a soul level. She was to help him learn important lessons in reliance, and he was helping her learn about love.

"When you told me that, I felt a surge go through me—a surge of remembrance. It was like I had a sudden consciousness of my purpose," she said. "I decided that if this was my job, I'd embrace it. I found that Simon is like a reflection of my moods. The happier I am, the happier he is. He chose a mom who won't drown in unhappiness. Understanding that has made it all much easier."

I asked her what else she'd learned from being with Simon. "Staying present—without a doubt," she said. "If you humor him or pretend to give him attention, he'll wallop you. You can't fool him!"

For anyone who can't take care of themselves, the advantage connected with a mission of Reliance is dependence, where they allow others to care for them. The risk, obduracy, can be seen in those who desperately need help, but can't let go of responsibility for themselves.

Next we're going to explore the mission Jennifer chose to help her through this challenging lifetime.

The Mission of Love
Advantage: Compassion
Risk: Ingratiation

A mission of Love is about learning to become a compassionate human being. By continually colliding with issues related to love, people on this mission get the chance to discover the importance of love.

They exude warmth and friendliness. They'll welcome you into their home, they'll make sure you're comfortable, and they'll want to get to know you better.

Their need for love in their lives is a two-way street. They want to both give and receive. What their souls seem to be saying is, "I love you; please love me."

The risk is that they may try too hard to be liked, by ingratiating themselves to others. Paradoxically, the harder they try, the more likely they are to push people away by appearing insecure, needy, or even insincere.

Theresa is on a mission of Love. "It's something I feel all around me," she said. "The problem is that because I'm so full of love, men often get the wrong idea. All through my life, I've had to deal with guys suddenly hitting on me."

During the session, we talked about some of the mixed signals she was giving out. As a very open and friendly person, Theresa exudes an air of empathy. But she also has the ingratiation that commonly results from the desire to be accepted by others.

I helped Theresa choose a new lawyer to better deal with her child custody issues. She called me a week or two later. I asked how the new lawyer was working out. She giggled nervously and said, "It was fine until yesterday. I was sitting in his office when he started hitting on me. I didn't know what to do."

What is she doing to attract all this unwanted attention? The underlying issue is her need to be loved. Her lack of self-acceptance makes her feel she has to appear "extra nice" in order to be accepted.

Theresa agreed. "All my life I've struggled to accept myself. I've never felt confident about my weight or appearance. It's only now that I'm finally coming to grips with who I am."

By trying too hard, she is seen by men in particular as flirtatious. The cure is to learn to accept herself for who she is.

The advantage associated with a mission of Love is compassion. It's a goal that may take many years and a great deal of effort to achieve, but the spiritual rewards are enormous.

Determine Your Mission

The following statements will help you to work out which of the ten missions you're on. Remember, there are two. Your primary mission is usually the stronger and will affect others, while your secondary mission is usually less outwardly noticeable but will have a more personal impact. (And, don't forget, if Connection is your primary mission, you'll have two secondary missions, the second of which floats.)

Enter into a meditative state (see page 14), and call in your spirit guides. Ask them to help you identify your missions. Use the following reminders of the advantages and risks to help you.

Change: The desire to move the world forward; the search for
   novelty

Exploration: The desire for first-hand knowledge; the urge to
   do everything

Examination: The need to understand how the world works;
   difficulty making decisions

Flow: The ability to accept life as it unfolds; the failure to grasp
   opportunities

Control: The desire to assert control or lead; reluctance to take
   advice

Connection: The desire for intimacy and deep relationships;
   overidentification with others

Avoidance: The desire for tranquility; the tendency to become
   insular

Healing: The desire to make yourself or others complete; becoming fixated on helping another person

Reliance: The need to depend on others; the refusal to accept
   help

Love: The need to give and receive love; the tendency to try too
   hard to be liked

Primary Mission:_____

Secondary Mission/s:_____

Still in a meditative state, call in your spirit guides. Ask them to support
you in embracing your missions. Repeat the following:

*"I call upon my spirit guides, acting in my highest interest, to help me
embrace my missions and allow me to live the life my soul intended."*

When you've finished, thank your spirit guides and tell them,
"Session over."

If you can identify and embrace your missions, you'll take a giant leap along your soul's evolutionary path. You'll be rewarded for your efforts by the sense of contentment that comes from your Physical Plane self and your soul walking hand in hand into a more purposeful future.

• • •

Now that you have your soul age, your soul type, and your missions, you have everything you need to live the life your soul intended.

Don't you?

Not quite. At this point, you've gained an understanding about the nature of your soul and why it chose to be here. But that's just one part of the picture.

As you continue on your journey, you're about to pass through the Door to Recovery, into a region of the Soul World where you'll discover how your soul's past affects the life you're living now.

PART 2: EMPOWERMENT

5: THE DOOR TO RECOVERY
Fears: Healing Past-Life Damage

*Past-life fears lurk beneath the surface of every individual. They are
a reminder of the soul's past, and how each life affects another.*
—THE AUTHOR'S CAUSAL GUIDES

Desperately trying to make himself heard above the jeers and
threats of a hostile mob, a father pleads for his son's life.
Amid the drama that's unfolding, tears of frustration stream down
his face as the terrifying reality hits him: what will happen next is
inevitable. Nothing he can say or do will prevent it.

A sneering official, whose dialect the father finds almost incom-
prehensible, steps forward and passes judgment. The crime: the theft
of an apple from a market stall. The sentence: imprisonment and
death for both father and son.

The location is a town in southern Italy during the time of the
Roman Empire. The father is a merchant who took his son with
him on a business trip to find a market for his metalware. After his
son stole a single piece of fruit, the locals apprehended him and
summoned the militia in charge of the city. Their officer saw the
opportunity to demonstrate his ruthlessness (and also to get his hands
on the merchant's valuable samples).

As they're hauled out of the room, the boy hysterical with
fear, the father's overwhelming emotion is one of injustice. The

feeling is compounded by a sense of failure at having been unable to protect his son.

Forty-something lifetimes later, the father is now a woman, and a talented jazz singer. In her present incarnation, the trauma from this past life has surfaced in the form of performance anxiety.

For almost every person who suffers from stage fright, a fear of public speaking, or who goes to pieces when forced to sit an exam, the root cause is a life in which judgment has led to death. When they're faced with a situation in which their soul senses that it's being judged, it reacts with a fight-or-flight response.

The Door to Recovery opens into the past, where traumatic events from your soul's previous incarnations are brought into the present to be confronted.

Past-life fears and phobias pop up when a trigger, an event in this lifetime, acts as a reminder. Like all fears, they're blocks to your soul's progress and, therefore, should be overcome if at all possible.

Someone once asked me, "If I've had lots of past lives, how come I don't remember them?" It's a good question. Here's what I told her:

You don't remember being two years old, either. At least, most of us don't. Yet if you were abused or neglected at that age, long-term damage will have been done—whether you can recall it or not.

The same goes for past lives. Events from other lifetimes are part of your soul's memory. And like childhood memories, it's usually the traumatic or unusual incidents that stand out.

What would happen if you could remember all your past lives? Would that help you in this one? The answer is no. The pain from this lifetime alone can be hard enough to deal with. Imagine how much worse it would be to remember all the grief and suffering from previous incarnations, too.

Having a clear recollection of everything that ever happened to you would be immobilizing. If you were killed in a car accident in your last incarnation, you might never learn to drive in this life.

Dorothy wanted to find out why her daughter suffers terrible separation anxiety when she leaves the house for work. It turned out that four-year-old Holly is terrified that she'll never see her mom again. The source of the fear is a lifetime they once shared in Nazi Germany.

This inspired Dorothy to explore other past lifetimes. Together, we went back to look at her last ten lives.

Her most recent life ended in Dachau concentration camp in Germany. In that lifetime, she was a young man, married to the woman who is now her daughter.

In the previous lifetime, Dorothy was a young Japanese sailor who died from shrapnel wounds to the abdomen in a battle at sea.

Before that, she was a Czech student in Bohemia who killed himself with poison rather than face compulsory military service.

During much of the nineteenth century, Dorothy was a woman in a community that later became a cooperative in India. Being psychic, she was feared by her employers, who strangled her in her sleep.

In the lifetime before that, she was a young man in the English county of Devon, who married his girlfriend against her father's wishes. After the father retaliated by mutilating his face, the young man fled the area, ending up in the Navy, where he died of scurvy at age thirty-five.

Dorothy was a German priest in the lifetime we looked at next. He was strangled and disemboweled by a group of religious reformers who were angered by his refusal to renounce his religion.

When the uprising of Uruguayan peasants he'd instigated failed, Dorothy, again male, died in prison after being turned in by his paternal grandmother, who hated him for his resemblance to the husband she hated.

As a pioneer farmer in Quebec, her husband stabbed her to death for her inheritance.

In Holland in the late 1500s, she was a boy who lost his parents around the age of five. He went to live with relatives in the mountains of Austria, and died of measles after a long and happy life.

In the last lifetime we explored, Dorothy was a young French-man who died on the first night of his visit to relatives in the Border region of Scotland. He'd just settled down for the evening, when he was reluctantly dragged into a fight with neighboring cattle thieves. By morning, he had bled to death.

My initial reaction was that Dorothy's last ten incarnations seemed unusually full of hardship and dramatic death. I asked my Causal guides for their opinion and they said, "The history of the world is brutal, and often lives are short and tragic. Dorothy's lives are unusual only in that she suffered death through disease in just two of ten incarnations."

And you may be interested to know that during the span of these ten lives, Dorothy had several brief incarnations in which she died in infancy.

It's purely coincidental, by the way, that most of her recent lives have been as a male. We all bounce from gender to gender and loca-tion to location as we progress through our lives on Earth.

Confronting the Past

A client once asked me, "Why isn't my soul smart enough to tell the dif-ference between this life and those in the past?"

To put it simply, your soul doesn't die. You may see your time on the Physical Plane as lots of lifetimes interspersed with periods spent in what we call death. Your soul sees it as one continuous experience.

There is no gender in the Soul World. Nor is there a sense of physical death being anything other than temporary.

From its first life to its last, your soul is conscious; its entire chain of lives is one continuous line. Like a line on a heart monitor, however, it has peaks that stand out. These are its death experiences. Most past-life fears that surface are related to how you felt about your life at the time of death.

The advantage associated with each past-life fear is your soul's goal, and, once achieved, it will act to release the grip the fear has on you. The risk is the result of avoiding tackling the fear.

The Ten Past-Life Fears

- The fear of Loss
- The fear of Betrayal
- The fear of Intimacy
- The fear of Rejection
- The fear of Self-Expression
- The fear of Authority
- The fear of Inferiority
- The fear of Powerlessness
- The fear of Failure
- The fear of Death

Many people have experienced past lives through regression therapy. Skeptics point out that the subject will be asked when the lifetime was, and answer something like, "The twelfth century." "How would this medieval peasant have known the date?" the skeptics will argue.

The subject knows the date because the experience is not being recalled from some little-known part of the brain; it's being channeled from the Soul World. (This is the reason relaxation is so important before undergoing regression.)

It's also why the past lives that come up are relevant to issues in this particular life, such as re-experiencing a trial and execution for witchcraft to help overcome a fear of authority.

The following stories show how traumatic experiences from previous lifetimes surface in often quite predictable ways. Most of the information that follows was channeled by me on behalf of a client, rather than by the client under regression.

The Fear of Loss
Advantage: Sufficiency
Risk: Uncertainty

Roughly a century ago, Molly was a young mother who lived in a Russian village with her extended family. She was in the woods when enemy troops came through the district, burning crops as they went. She hid and watched in horror as the soldiers torched the village and slaughtered her family.

When she came out of hiding, she discovered her baby had been burned to death in their home. She died soon after from the effects of starvation and grief.

In this lifetime, Molly is an alternative healer who lives a comfortable lifestyle in northern California. She has a loving husband and three great kids. Yet, she's terrified of losing everything.

The fear isn't specific. She can't say it's just a fear of losing her family or her home. What she's dealing with is a deep sense of life being unpredictable.

"I try to harden myself by imagining the worst so it won't be such a shock when it happens," she said. "I tell myself that if they all die and I'm left behind, I'll be okay."

No matter how secure Molly's life really is, she never feels she can trust it to last. Her fear of Loss gives her a sense of uncertainty; she fears that everything she has could evaporate due to circumstances beyond her control.

The advantage is sufficiency, the awareness that she has everything she needs, which is, in fact, all she needs to put this fear behind her. The risk, should she choose to do nothing, will continue to be uncertainty.

The Fear of Betrayal

Advantage: Loyalty
Risk: Mistrust

In a previous life, Ray was struggling to keep his restaurant going. He'd gambled away his profits and was in serious debt. Then along came a business partner who offered to pay off his debts in exchange for ownership of the business. He promised to keep Ray on—and pay him a good salary, too.

Ray couldn't believe his luck. He signed the business over to his partner and waited for the money. It never came. When he went to the authorities, his partner convinced them that he'd given Ray the money, but he'd gambled it away.

Ray died in poverty, bitter to the end about how he'd been conned.

In this lifetime, Ray is charming and outgoing. He appears to have plenty of confidence, yet the fear of betrayal is always close to the surface.

Is Ray my client? No, my client is actually Sandra, his business partner in the clothing store he owns.

Ray was ready to open a second outlet when Sandra discovered she was pregnant. She announced that after she gave birth, she planned to quit work and stay home to raise the baby.

Ray was furious. He accused Sandra of deserting him when he needed her most. Even after his initial rage had died down, he wouldn't talk to her or acknowledge her presence. She was deeply upset by his reaction, and wondered what she'd done to offend him.

Sandra's behavior was perfectly normal, and there was nothing she could have done to predict or prevent the severity of Ray's reaction. The problem was entirely his.

The risk in the case of a fear of Betrayal is mistrust. If he were ever to overcome his fear of Betrayal, it would be through the development of its advantage, which is loyalty. By doing this, he would stand a much greater chance of receiving the loyalty of others.

The Fear of Intimacy

Advantage: Trust
Risk: Inhibition

Abby has always struggled with intimacy problems in this life. She's never felt comfortable with any of her partners, and this has been the cause of two divorces. Now in her sixties, she describes herself as someone who's never really known happiness. Her life, she told me, has been one of continual loneliness.

The source of her fears turned out to be a short lifetime of abuse in a remote farm in Sweden during the 1800s.

In what was an extremely harsh life, Abby was a young girl who was constantly sexually abused by her male relatives. In her mid-teens, she escaped the misery by starving herself to death.

In her present life, the memory of her ordeal in Sweden is still with her. Not surprisingly, being treated as an object rather than a human being created a lack of self-worth in Abby's present life. Not only does she have intimacy issues, she's also extremely overweight—something which is directly related to the way she died.

If you've suffered abuse in a past life, it will, at some point, come to the surface so it can be worked through and eradicated. The advantage, trust, is the cure. Not confronting the fear leads to the risk, which is inhibition.

The Fear of Rejection

Advantage: Intimacy
Risk: Insularity

Midori is a young Japanese-American woman with a three-year-old daughter. They live like hermits, rarely venturing out into the world. When they do leave their home, Midori keeps her daughter in her arms or at her side constantly.

During her session, a past life came up. She had been a young woman in Korea in the mid-1900s. At that time, she became friendly with a Japanese soldier, who ultimately got her pregnant. She was thrown out by her family for bringing shame to the household.

That lifetime ended for Midori when, alone in a field, she bled to death during childbirth. She died feeling unloved, lonely, and despised.

At that point, Midori experienced what it was like to be abandoned by those close to her. The fear was given an added dimension by feelings of having abandoned her newborn baby.

The fear of Rejection has left her reluctant to put trust in anyone in this life. It's just "too risky." She sees herself as self-sufficient and independent. Sadly, the reality is that her fear prevents her from experiencing intimacy with anyone but her daughter. She has fallen into the risk, which is insularity.

Those who are diagnosed with "abandonment issues" in this lifetime are often dealing with a fear of Rejection. A child who bursts into tears when he loses sight of Mom in the supermarket, or a woman who fears every lover she has will leave her, may have been abandoned in a previous incarnation.

The advantage, should Midori choose to overcome her resistance to change, is intimacy. By allowing herself to experience intimacy with others, she'd soon overcome the fear that has become such a huge part of her life and that of her daughter.

The Fear of Self-Expression

Advantage: Self-Acceptance
Risk: Sycophancy

This next lifetime also took place in the Far East. Andrea, who is an accountant in this life, was a prostitute in a bordello in Japan. Day after day, she had to pretend to be nice to customers she hated.

When one man began beating her sadistically, she dropped her pretense and told him how much he revolted her. He took out his deep-rooted hatred of women on her, and beat her savagely until she died.

At the time of her death, Andrea experienced huge feelings of anger at having had to keep up an act, all the time hating her customers for what she was forced to do.

In this incarnation, she struggles with speaking out or letting others know how she really feels. Her soul remembers what happened that last time she expressed her true feelings.

The way her fear manifests itself is that she acts, as she put it, "like a chameleon." Nobody knows the real Andrea because she molds her personality according to the person she's with.

"My conservative friends think I'm conservative, and my liberal friends think I'm liberal," she said. "The most ridiculous thing I've done was to pretend to be a Catholic even though I was raised Lutheran. I can't go back to that hairdresser because she kept asking me awkward questions about which church I go to and who I know. It's so embarrassing!"

The risk, sycophancy, results in a person telling others what they think they want to hear. The advantage is simply a matter of self-acceptance, and learning, on a soul level, that voicing your opinions will not put your survival in jeopardy.

The Fear of Authority

Advantage: Equality
Risk: Inferiority

After being found guilty (despite his actual innocence) of plotting against one of the Hapsburg kings, Frank was tortured and eventually strangled. At death, his belief was that authority is inherently unjust.

In this lifetime, Frank's heart would start beating wildly at the mere sight of a police officer, and he used to hate going through customs even though he had nothing to hide.

As Frank learned to develop the advantage, equality, his issues with authority figures quickly evaporated. Had he not done so, he might still be stuck with the risk, inferiority, which had been with him since childhood, and had turned schoolteachers into intimidating symbols of power.

A reminder of his death by strangulation is the problem Frank encounters when talking to people in positions of authority: he finds great difficulty in swallowing, and sometimes even loses his voice.

The Fear of Inferiority
Advantage: Self-Confidence
Risk: Jealousy

A feeling of inferiority is only made possible by having a soul that's able to compare and contrast. Many people can compare and contrast without experiencing envy, but when there is resentment from a past life, unexplained jealousy can arise.

Julia is a young assistant in the production department of a major New York advertising agency. Her problem is that she can't control her jealousy of people around her. "I'm a bitch!" she told me. "And I've always been that way. I don't know what gets into me, but it's like I can't bear to see anyone else happy."

In the absence of any present-life cause, we went back several lifetimes to Renaissance Italy, when Julia was the mistress of a great artist.

She had no problems with jealousy in that life, despite the fact that her lover was married with quite a number of children. But when he and his family relocated to another country, she was left behind, and became resentful and bitter.

When the artist died a few years later, Julia was grief-stricken. Despite her anger at what she felt was his infidelity, she'd never stopped loving him.

Comparing herself to the artist's wife gave her deep feelings of inferiority. He had, after all, chosen to be with the other woman.

A reminder of her previous lifetime is with Julia every time she compares someone else's happiness to her own.

By working on developing self-confidence, even the most green-eyed person can overcome the past-life emotions that cause them to compare themselves unfavorably to others. This will help them avoid the risk, which is, of course, jealousy.

The Fear of Powerlessness

Advantage: Flexibility
Risk: Intransigence

In Wendy's past is a life spent in Northern Ireland. She was a young boy, an orphan, who worked in a linen mill. This lifetime ended tragically after an accident at work broke both his legs. With little education and no longer able to do heavy work, he became a beggar. He was killed in a fight over a penny, and died feeling he'd never had any self-determination in that life.

In this life, Wendy has not only a fear of Powerlessness, but also a mission of Control. As a result, she's continually forced to confront issues of power and control in her work and domestic life. After a lifetime of feeling like a victim of circumstance, she has a tendency to go a little too much the other way in this one.

Control Freaks

We often use the derogatory term "control freak" to describe an individual who seems to have the need for control over people, his or her own self, or their environment.

Perhaps if we understood that this person might well be struggling with intransigence, the risk associated with the fear of Powerlessness, we'd show them a little more sympathy.

Negotiating pay with her boss risked damaging their relationship until my spirit guides encouraged Wendy to be willing to make a few concessions. The risk, intransigence, can be hard to overcome, but doing so leads to the advantage, flexibility, which allows an individual to exercise self-determination without becoming oblivious to the needs of others.

The Fear of Failure

Advantage: Patience
Risk: Urgency

A fear of Failure follows a lifetime, and sometimes several lifetimes, in which a person has died before they've had a chance to complete their life plan.

Alan is one such person.

In 1940, just a year into World War II, he was a seven-year-old boy in Berlin. In one of the first British air raids, he and his older sister were killed. Though the young boy didn't consciously know it, he was supposed to grow up and be a doctor.

Between that life and this, he had another unexpectedly short incarnation. These experiences have left him with a fear that he might not complete this life either.

As a doctor in this life, Alan is involved in groundbreaking research, which he's doing with the utmost integrity. He's not in it for the glory; he's simply driven to help others. He's always known he was meant to make life better for other people.

"When I was seven years old, I saw a TV program showing starving African children," he told me. "I got a really strong urge to help. Then, when I was eight, I decided to become a doctor."

A fear of Failure creates a feeling of not having enough time. "Do you worry about not getting the chance to finish your research in this lifetime?" I asked him.

"Worry?" Alan said. "I've actually experienced panics when I think about dying before I complete my life's work."

Though Alan fears not completing his life plan, he has no fear of death itself. As a Level 7 soul, he's done it many times before.

Alan has worked successfully to overcome the risk associated with this fear, and that's urgency. When we first met, Alan was one of the most impatient clients I've encountered. Now he's a different person. By embracing the advantage, patience, he's learning to let life unfold at its own pace.

The Fear of Death
Advantage: Acceptance
Risk: Phobia

Death lies at the root of many seemingly unrelated fears. Under regression, Eric discovered the source of his fear of loneliness. He found himself back in a lifetime in Greece, where he died beside a lake. As his soul left his body, the feeling that overwhelmed him was that of being alone. He wished he could have died at home with his family around him.

Shirley once had a life in which she worked in the engine room of a small boat sailing out of Hamburg. Due to her lack of care, the boiler exploded, killing several crew members. In this lifetime, she has a huge fear of making even the smallest mistake. On a soul level, there is a belief that her bad judgment might have tragic consequences and could even result in her death or that of others.

Triggers

You might get bitten by a dog when you're three years old, and be afraid of dogs as a result. But the incident is not likely to create a full-blown phobia.

In fact, a childhood trauma, like being attacked by a dog, is usually not so much a cause as a trigger—a reminder of something that happened in another incarnation.

Phobias fall into the fear of Death category, since that's always the underlying cause. In this section, we're going to examine the ten most common phobias, which, like the other fears we've looked at, are related to past lives.

Though we all tend to lose a fear of our own mortality as our souls age, an incident from the past can bring a fear of death into anyone's life.

Carole has always had a fear of being submerged in water. At school, she was forced to jump into the deep end of the pool. "The other kids were fine, but I started bobbing up and down and drowning, and the teacher had to jump in and rescue me," she said. "I've always had real problems in the water. I still do. I've had more swimming lessons than anyone you know."

During a regression, she went back to a lifetime as a man who died in tragic circumstances.

"I see woods and meadows," she said softly. "There is a lake . . . I live off the land . . . I'm fishing on my own. It looks like I'm wearing a lot of clothes . . . heavy, rough leather . . . " As she spoke, her hands began to tremble and her cheeks flushed.

"I feel myself falling into the water . . . my boots, my clothes, are full of water and dragging me down . . . I'm sinking . . . trying to get to the surface . . . "

I asked her what was going through her mind while this was happening. "I have a fear of drowning . . . I know I'm drowning . . . " she gasped.

At that point, I took Carole ahead to the very moment her soul left her body. "What are your feelings about this life you've just had?" I asked.

"I feel so sad . . . I worked so hard to survive . . . I feel sadness at leaving people behind."

Regression is often used as a way to help people overcome their fears, and that appears to have been the case with Carole. Almost a year after this session, she was in a canoe in Puget Sound with her husband and a friend when it capsized.

"It was just like that past life," she said. "I felt myself being dragged down, and I started to panic. But I was wearing a life vest. As soon as I realized I wasn't going under, I was okay. It took us about twenty minutes to swim to shore. By the time we got there, I was actually able to laugh about it."

Irrational Fears

We use the term "irrational fear" to describe a phobia. For your soul, however, it all seems perfectly rational. When it suddenly encounters a trigger, its reaction is, "Oh my God! Remember what happened the last time we encountered this?" (And the answer is: "We died!")

A fear of Death is not always a phobia. But a phobia is always a fear of Death.

Each of the ten major phobias has a past-life origin, as well as present-life triggers that cause it to surface.

The Ten Past-Life Phobias

- Loss of Control
- Open Spaces
- Sickness
- Enclosed Spaces
- Strangers
- Darkness
- The Unknown
- Judgment
- Water
- Heights

Your soul's fears are related to its emotional state at the time of death. Understanding what happens on a soul level is the key to overcoming phobias. The advantage is the cure, and it can be described as the acceptance that the object of the fear will not cause your death. The risk is, not surprisingly, phobia.

The following is a list of the ten categories that cover the most common soul-influenced irrational fears.

Phobia of Loss of Control

When there has been no self-determination at the time of death (being ordered into battle, for example), the soul will fear situations that are beyond its control. The triggers can be dentists, flying, or even panic itself.

Phobia of Open Spaces

A phobia of open spaces is created when the soul leaves the body without sufficient attachment to the Astral Plane, because of the effects of drugs, medication, or even the inability to accept death. The soul finds itself in limbo, stuck between this plane and the next.

Before reaching the Astral Plane, the soul will have the opportunity to experience its own immensity and that of the universe, which, if it's unprepared, can be terrifying and make it want to withdraw. It must lose its connection to the Physical Plane before finding its way to the Astral Plane.

The triggers are open spaces, crowds, and heights.

Phobia of Sickness

Dying of disease before its life plan has been completed results in the soul believing that sickness will lead to death. The triggers are blood, vomiting, doctors, hospitals, and other reminders of illness.

Phobia of Enclosed Spaces

This next phobia is also found among those souls who have had difficulties leaving the Physical Plane behind. If the soul was still present when its physical body was buried (and this has nothing to do with being buried alive), it will associate the experience with death.

When faced with triggers, such as being restrained or being confined, it will be reminded of the past, creating a feeling of panic.

Phobia of Strangers

Though a mistrust or fear of those from different cultures is common in younger souls, a genuine phobia of strangers is caused by a death in the presence of foreigners, often on the battlefield. (The soul is much more comfortable dying in the presence of family, friends, or familiar faces.) The triggers are racial characteristics, foreign accents and unusual facial features.

Phobia of Darkness

The phobia of darkness is a genuine phobia that is very visceral. It has its roots in the experience of being in a coma or becoming unconscious before death. One of its manifestations is a fear of losing consciousness in a public place, and is associated with a past life in which the soul has been helpless prior to death.

The triggers are, not surprisingly, darkness, but can also be the sensation of fainting or feeling "outside your body."

Phobia of the Unknown

We've already seen how, when the soul dies and "goes toward the light," it may find itself lost in the space between this plane and the Astral Plane. This may not happen often, but when it does the trauma is immense.

While lost, a younger soul with few deaths behind it is the one most likely to experience the overwhelming fear that there is nothing beyond the Physical Plane.

The triggers are unfamiliar situations, which the soul associates with death.

Phobia of Judgment

When the soul has died as a result of harsh or unfair judgment, it will react with fear to triggers such as public speaking, performance, or taking exams. It is concerned that the past experience will be repeated, and that the result will be a death sentence.

The reason a phobia of judgment appears to be so common is that there are continual triggers, many of them unavoidable. The one that gives the most people the greatest anxiety is talking in public, but even mild social anxiety can have its roots in a phobia of judgment.

Judgment in a past life may have been in front of a courtroom—a trial for witchcraft, for example—but in a world like ours, there are many more common causes of this phobia.

With our tragic history of religious and ethnic persecution, millions of us have perished in massacres and pogroms, having been judged to be lesser human beings than others.

Phobia of Water

As we saw with Carole, a past life in which you drowned can come back to haunt you in a future lifetime. It's no surprise that the trigger is water.

Many people who have died in this way have found themselves suspended between this and the Astral Plane, which can sometimes lead to the next phobia on the list.

Phobia of Heights

Dying in a car crash, getting blown up, or being killed in battle can come as a surprise, however much the conscious mind may be prepared for such an eventuality.

In fact, any sudden or violent separation of the soul from the body can cause the soul to fear being disconnected from the Physical Plane. Like the phobias of both open spaces and water, this fear is also connected with being caught between planes.

The trigger for this phobia is height, which reminds the soul that being separated from the Physical Plane leads to death.

Visceral Fears

Not all seemingly irrational fears are true phobias. Some, like a fear of hypodermic needles, spiders, snakes and even birds, are visceral—part of our hardwiring.

• • •

Past-life fears are to be dealt with, not ignored. Since they act as blocks to your spiritual evolution, it's in your highest interest to confront and overcome them. If you don't deal with them in this lifetime, you'll simply have to do so in another.

Assuming you don't want to be dragging these reminders of

your soul's past around with you all your life, the following technique will help you eradicate your fear or fears, in a manner that you may find entertaining.

Identify and Annihilate Your Past-Life Fears

You may have one or several fears. It's important to tackle them one at a time. The first step in defeating any fear is to figure out exactly what it is. The second step is to annihilate it. This is where you show your fear who's boss.

Let's begin. Enter a meditative state (see page 14), and call in your spirit guides. Ask them to support you as you carry out the following exercise.

Step 1: Identify Your Fear

Use the following list to help you determine which past-life fears you've brought into this life.

The fear of Loss: The belief that everything could be gone tomorrow

The fear of Betrayal: The feeling that people always let you down

The fear of Intimacy: A reluctance to get too emotionally or physically close to others

The fear of Rejection: The belief that getting too close to someone will cause them to leave

The fear of Self-Expression: The tendency to act differently depending on who you're with

The fear of Authority: Discomfort with people in uniforms or figures of authority

The fear of Inferiority: Jealousy of those who appear to be happier than you

The fear of Powerlessness: A determination to run your own life

The fear of Failure: Worry that there is insufficient time to achieve your goals

The fear of Death: Having a phobia

Fear of:_____

Step 2: Annihilate Your Fear

Still in a meditative state, ask your spirit guides to help you annihilate your fear.

Stand facing the bathroom mirror, look straight into your eyes, and tell your fear you're not going to put up with it any longer. Show it no mercy. (Imagine you're a professional wrestler railing against your opponent.)

Here's how to do it:

"Listen up, Fear of _____!
I've had it with you, you little punk! I'm going to murder you. I'm going to be your assassin. You'd better get out of here while you have the chance. I'm done with you. I want you gone . . . NOW! I will annihilate you . . . " And so on.

When you've finished, thank your spirit guides and tell them, "Session over."

Give yourself a couple of minutes several times a day to do this exercise. If you have more than one fear, wait until you notice a shift in the first before you move on to the next.

The exact words don't matter as long as you identify the fear by name. If you're dealing with a phobia, identify it if you can; otherwise, call it simply a fear of Death. Your soul and your spirit guides will know what to do.

You don't have to yell—you can grit your teeth and hiss the words through them. Use emotive words. Have fun with it. If you can't do it in front of a mirror, do it while you're stuck in traffic or somewhere quiet.

Be cautious about using words like "assassin" and "annihilate" in public places. You don't want to get arrested!

If your fears are mild, or if you really can't bring yourself to take such an aggressive approach, there is a less dramatic way to deal with these negative past-life issues. Again, it requires a short meditation. Call in your guides and make the following request:

"I call upon my spirit guides, acting in my highest interest, to help me overcome my past-life fears to allow me to live the life my soul intended."

Don't forget to thank your guides and tell them, "Session over."

· · ·

At the beginning of this chapter, I told you about a singer who suffered terribly from performance anxiety. After exploring her past life and using the "annihilation" technique, she was gradually able to conquer her fear and get back to performing again.

Now, as we move more into your soul's present, we'll investigate another obstacle to living the life your soul intended that's so heavily disguised many of us don't even recognize it—yet almost all of us run into it at one time or another.

6: THE DOOR TO BALANCE
Desires: Avoiding False Goals

Desires are the result of earthly influences, not part of the soul's true purpose, and are detrimental to an individual's life plan.
—THE AUTHOR'S CAUSAL GUIDES

E very one of us comes here with a life plan. Yet sticking to it can be hard. That's why this next door leads to a place where you can learn to balance your very human cravings with your soul's need for you to stick to your life plan.

Your soul wants you to stay focused on what you came here to do, which means avoiding the many diversions that get in your way. And that takes us through the Door to Balance, to confront something called Desires: false goals that may take you well off your chosen life plan.

Pinocchio's False Goal

Remember how Pinocchio got sidetracked? All he had to do was get to school. Yet within minutes of leaving home, he was in a bar surrounded by ruffians, smoking a cigar and playing pool.

His goal was school. His desire, his false goal, was Glamour.

Alas, Pinocchio is not alone. We all get sidetracked at some point or another. Some of us spend our entire lives following our desires rather than our missions. The result can be a kind of spiritual stagnation, as our soul finds itself unable to progress in this lifetime.

Desires are rooted in the Physical Plane, not the Soul World, which is why they have no spiritual value. How often have you heard that money doesn't buy happiness? Don't we all know that rank and status are ultimately quite meaningless?

But what about education or health? Surely they're desirable desires? Of course they are. But then, all desires are—in moderation.

The advantage associated with any desire is what your soul *really* wants, and is achieved by balancing the desire so that it no longer interferes with your life plan. The risk is the unfortunate effect of embracing the desire, and prevents spiritual growth. As we explore each of the ten desires, you'll see how they can be hypnotic in their appeal, but damaging when they get out of balance.

The Ten Desires

- The desire for Safety
- The desire for Wealth
- The desire for Education
- The desire for Glamour
- The desire for Attraction
- The desire for Status
- The desire for Health
- The desire for Power
- The desire for Fame
- The desire for Immortality

The Desire for Safety

Advantage: Achievement
Risk: Immobilization

Confucius once said, "A ship in the harbor is safe—but that's not what ships are for."

A desire for Safety prevents you from achieving all the goals your soul has planned for this lifetime. And, though you may feel comfortable in the safety of your own personal harbor, if you're going to fulfill your life plan, it's important to get out into the world and take a few risks.

One of my clients, Hannah, seemed like the least likely candidate for having a desire for Safety. She'd just given up her husband and her home, and was about to fly out, that same week, to New Guinea, where she'd be working for an AIDS charity.

"I spent my entire life searching for safety," she said. "I married a boring man and took a really dull job, all because I wanted security."

So, what changed? When her children left home, Hannah (a Level 10 Thinker with a Spiritualist influence and missions of Connection and Change) looked at her life and decided it was not what she wanted. She saw through the Illusion and realized her future was going to be all about helping people less fortunate than herself.

Most of us know what it's like to be afraid of the unknown. But when it gets out of balance, the desire for Safety can be immobilizing. Instead of taking a chance like Hannah did, many people prefer to cling to the illusion of certainty that this desire offers.

And it is just an illusion. Was Hannah happy with her unexciting life? Absolutely not. It took many years for her to cast aside the risk, immobilization, and launch herself into the uncertain yet exciting advantage of achievement. Her life is now one in which she's on her way to finding profound fulfillment by living the life her soul intended.

The Desire for Wealth

Advantage: Opportunity
Risk: Materialism

This is the most common desire of all. What's wrong with wanting money? Nothing. We all need it to survive. Problems arise, however, when you want it so much that it takes you off your life plan.

Denise asked me for help in a matter that actually concerned her husband. Several years before, Ron had gone into business with a pair of crooks who'd used his money and credibility to buy rental property in Miami.

Ron had known nothing about real estate, but was lured by the promise of easy money with very little effort. In a complex fraud, his partners took his investment and bilked him out of his share of the business.

With right on his side, Ron had sued his ex-partners. Unfortunately, it hadn't gone well. The legal process had taken years, cost Ron a fortune, and looked like it would drag on for a long time to come. Worse still, his partners had turned the tables on him. There was a real risk he might actually lose the case. The stress was eating him up.

As I was talking to Denise, I suddenly found myself in the presence of Ron's father.

"I have Ron's dad with me," I said.

"Oh my gosh!" Denise squealed. "Ask him what he thinks. Ron always trusted his advice when his dad was alive."

The message was clear. "It's killing him," Ron's father said. "Tell him to walk away from it and get back to what's really important." (What was important was taking care of his family. One of the lessons Ron was learning was that money doesn't replace love.)

Denise agreed. "I keep telling him it'll kill him, but he's like a man possessed."

My guides came back in and gave their two cents' worth. They said that Ron's desire for Wealth was blinding him to reality. He felt a deep sense of injustice, which was hardly surprising. But it was his desire that had not only led him into this sordid business, but was also keeping him locked in a battle he was unlikely to win.

Happiness is elusive when we're more focused on making money than following our life plans. Underlying a desire for Wealth is a need for the opportunity that wealth offers. But when the desire gets out of balance, it turns to materialism, the risk, which blocks the path to spirituality.

The Desire for Education

Advantage: Knowledge
Risk: Procrastination

What on earth could possibly be wrong with education? Usually nothing. Most of us don't get nearly as much as we could use. But sometimes, enough is enough.

While education leads to the advantage, knowledge, an out-of-balance desire for it can function as a distraction; it's a way to put off actually living the life your soul intended.

You see it in people who become "permanent students," always going from one course to the next. They're constantly learning, but never doing anything with it.

In Carrie's case, the last thing her soul wanted was another year at school.

As the summer neared an end and college loomed on the horizon, she became increasingly miserable. She simply didn't know whether to go back or not.

The answer wasn't hard to find. What was ailing this Creator type was the thought of going back to art school to complete her final year rather than seizing some incredible opportunities that had come her way. She sat down opposite me, close to tears.

"I've been asked to illustrate a children's book, some posters, and all sorts of other projects that are coming my way," she told me. "The problem is I'm only a year away from getting my degree. One part of me feels that I can't give up now, but the other part dreads going back to school."

"Your career has already started," I told her. "What your soul wants now is for you to get on with your life. It doesn't need another year of college."

No matter how I asked my spirit guides the question, they saw no advantage to Carrie in going back to school. "If it helps her," they said, "remind her that she can always finish college sometime in the future."

That evening, Carrie's mother, Leslie, called to thank me. "I don't remember the last time I saw her this happy!" she said.

The next afternoon, however, Leslie called again. "It's a disaster!" she cried. "Carrie had lunch with the guy who helped her get into college. He's talked her into going back. Now she's unhappy and confused again."

She begged me to meet up with Carrie and convince her not to go. I explained that it's not my job to convince anyone of anything, but she was insistent.

So that evening, I met Carrie again for a chat. I told her the same thing I'd told her mom. "The answer from my spirit guides isn't going to change in a day," I explained. "You're being guided not to go back to school, but ultimately it's your choice. Listen to your own intuition, and don't make your decision based on my guides' or anyone else's opinion."

As we spoke, Carrie broke into a smile. "I think I know what I have to do," she said.

It's been six months, and Carrie is working as a professional illustrator. The last time I saw her, I asked her how it was all working out. "I've just moved into a studio, and work keeps coming in," she said. "My life has never been better."

The Desire for Glamour
Advantage: Stimulation
Risk: Jadedness

When I had my first session with Heather, I told her she was just about to meet someone called Isabella. A day later, that's exactly what happened—though not quite in the way she expected. Isabella turned out to be a six-foot-six transvestite she ran into at a party.

After a trip to Burning Man, the annual festival held in the Black Rock Desert, Heather had thrown herself into its associated party scene.

"I've always been a rebel," she told me. "I was looking for an alternative lifestyle, and I found it through Burning Man."

Weekends became a blur of glamorous parties. "I'd stay awake for days, partying the whole time."

Then Heather started dating a guy who was doing heavy-duty drugs. "I loved acid," she said. "I'd always found it very alluring. And I'd started doing a lot of coke. But it all took an ugly turn when I met Gary. I got into crystal meth—real evil stuff. I realized I was losing control of my life."

One night, Gary was at the wheel of Heather's car when they skidded off the road and hit a tree. "We were high on crack, so we ran off as fast as we could. After that, I started to see the destruction around me, and what the drugs were doing to me. It wasn't fun anymore. I'd developed a real hard edge, and I'd started to lose my friends."

Heather's desire for Glamour had reached the point where the stimulation her fast lifestyle had once offered had turned into habit. And that was the point where her awareness allowed her soul to finally make its own desire felt.

It took her several years, but she finally put her destructive past behind her and found the alternative lifestyle she really needed: she moved from the city to a small town where she grows organic vegetables with her long-term boyfriend, a man almost thirty years younger than she is.

The Desire for Attraction

Advantage: Acceptance
Risk: Superficiality

Heather's not alone when it comes to her penchant for younger men. Celia has had a string of boyfriends half her age. What both these women have in common is a desire for Attraction: a fear of losing their youth and sexuality.

When I first met Celia, it was clear that what she really yearned for was someone she could spend the rest of her life with. Yet on the surface, she gave the appearance of wanting something else. From the way she dressed, spoke, and behaved, settling down seemed to be the last thing she wanted.

Celia has a number of fears. At the top of the list is a fear of aging. "I worry all the time about growing old and not being wanted," she confessed.

At an early age, girls in particular learn to use their sexuality to give themselves power. As they grow up, many place an exaggerated importance on physical looks and youth. Then, when they see signs of aging (Celia joked about applying her makeup with a trowel), a panic sets in. They assume that their desirability is entirely tied up with their appearance.

When she was younger, Celia worked as a waitress and bartender. Now she spends her evenings trying to hold onto her youth by hanging out in all her old haunts.

But by dressing like a teenager and getting wasted every night, she's sending out a mixed message. Her behavior is actually getting in the way of her real goal: finding a life partner.

Many people who have grown up unloved, or whose self-esteem is low, will use the desire for Attraction to be accepted. An unfortunate result of this desire is superficiality, forgetting that who they are goes way beyond their Physical Plane self.

The Desire for Status

Advantage: Respect
Risk: Self-Importance

There is an old Italian proverb that says, "At the end of the game, all the pieces go back in the same box."

It's a reminder that status is, in a spiritual sense, quite meaningless. It's only on this plane that it actually matters. You may be a VIP here on earth, but when you review your life on the Astral Plane, no one—least of all your soul—is going to care about the letters after your name, the rank you held, or which rung of the social ladder you ended up on.

The Desire for Status

The Buddha put it well when he said: "So what of all these titles, names, and races? They are mere worldly conventions."

Most people who actively seek out status do so because they want others to respect them. Unfortunately, they can't force people to look up to them. What they're most likely to end up with is simply an elevated sense of self-importance.

The way people with this desire can best achieve the advantage is to exercise their authority with integrity.

The Desire for Health

Advantage: Fitness
Risks: Hypochondria

What's wrong with being healthy? Nothing, of course—just as long as you retain a sense of perspective.

Audrey lost hers when she started working out at the gym in the basement of her Los Angeles apartment building. After a while, she started getting up earlier and earlier to fit in more running time before work. Soon she was spending her lunch hour at the gym, then running in the park after work. After dinner, she'd work out some more.

"It made me feel really alive. I began thinking of nothing else. I'd run through the mall where I could see myself reflected in the shop windows. It was an obsession. I became totally narcissistic," she said.

During that period, which lasted several years, Audrey became obsessed with her body. She was convinced that every little ache or pain was the sign of something much worse. She lost so much weight on a diet that she became sick.

Then she broke her ankle when she fell off a sidewalk, and the injury forced her to take a break. Soon she became seriously ill. During her convalescence, she saw how far over the top she'd gone.

When she recovered she worked on getting her desire for Health into balance with the rest of her life.

If your desire is Health, the advantage, fitness, is your soul's goal. As for the risk, if you've ever known a hypochondriac, you'll have seen what happens when an interest in the physical body and its functions get out of balance.

The Desire for Power
Advantage: Confidence
Risk: Arrogance

The desire for Power may look like a mission of Control, but there is one significant difference: the desire for Power is only ever seen in those who are fundamentally insecure about themselves. In an attempt to build confidence, they frequently use their power for selfish ends.

As world leaders, they'll attack other countries; as judges, they'll impose cruel and harsh sentences on those who are powerless. As parents or spouses, they'll rule through coercion and terror.

Sometimes an individual with a desire for Power will deliberately manipulate a situation to provoke a reaction. (It allows them to justify exerting their power.) Once they've initiated a response, they'll take stern measures, all of which are designed to make themselves look tough. They'll fire an entire workforce, invade another country, or use the courts as a weapon.

What their soul wants them to achieve is the advantage, confidence, and the ability to use a position of authority with responsibility. The risk is arrogance. From a distance, it may look like confidence, but it lacks spiritual substance.

The Desire for Fame

Advantage: Recognition
Risk: Transience

"I had my fifteen minutes of fame almost twenty years ago," Ursula told me. "It taught me a lesson I'll never forget."

It began with a talent show in her Midwest home town. Ursula had always dreamed of becoming famous. As a fourteen-year-old Performer type, she fantasized about strangers recognizing her, adoring fans asking for her autograph, and seeing herself on the front cover of magazines.

This was her big chance. She entered the talent contest performing a cover of a popular comic song.

"I was a hit!" she said. "People recognized me on the street. I had my picture in the papers. And it went to my head. From the way I acted, you'd have thought I was a Hollywood star!"

Over the next few weeks, Ursula played a few more concerts. She even did a spot on a local radio station. And that was it. Her brand new career came to a complete halt.

"By the time I was fifteen, I was a has-been," she joked. "I thought my next stop was the Johnny Carson show. It wasn't. It was back to school."

Ursula's story illustrates the point that it's those who deliberately seek out fame who have the least chance of a) finding it, or b) keeping it.

Fame is fickle—especially for those whose talent or ability fails to support their desire. It offers the reward of recognition, which many people, particularly Performers, crave. But its effect is transient. Not only is the public unpredictable, but the inherent worthlessness of fame becomes apparent as soon as the initial buzz wears off.

Just ask Ursula. "Once I realized how shallow fame really was, I began concentrating on my first love: playing the piano. Over the years I've had far more media attention doing that than I ever had from my silly songs. And I don't even have to try. I learned a powerful lesson back then. It's taught me to see fame for what it is, and not let it take me away from what I love doing."

The Desire for Immortality
Advantage: Achievement
Risk: Mortality

The idea that life continues after death can be a hard one to accept—especially for those who are caught up in the Illusion. Since they believe that life is a one-shot deal, they place great importance on leaving a lasting legacy.

"Remember Me When I'm Gone"

The desire for Immortality lies behind the need certain individuals have to write a book, make a record, achieve an Olympic gold medal, or even commit serial murder. (That's not to suggest, of course, that everyone who—ahem—writes a book does it for that reason.)

The positive benefit of a desire for Immortality is that it pushes people to achieve things they might not otherwise have done. Like fame, however, immortality is rarely achieved by those who actively seek it out. Just because you set out to write the great American novel doesn't mean you actually will. (The public will decide whether or not your novel is great.)

The desire for Immortality is most visible in powerful Level 5 leaders, since so many of them are unable to escape the Illusion, and as such believe that life is a one-shot deal. They raise monuments to themselves to trumpet their importance and ensure they won't be forgotten. In the past, pyramids, palaces, and statues were the preferred choice. These days, it's more likely to be a skyscraper or a sports stadium bearing the name of its wealthy founder.

Immortality is much more likely to come as a side effect of doing what you do best. The long-term impact you make is subject to the whims of fashion. And, of course, any concern you might have about immortality ends with your physical death.

Balancing Your Desires

Something all desires have in common is that the harder you try to achieve them, the more they'll elude you.

Desires are unfulfilling and often intangible. The object of the desire may never actually be reached. A desire for Education, for example, has no end. How do you know when you've got enough? Or take Glamour. What does too much look like?

The secret to overcoming desires is not to destroy them, but to master them. The way to do that is to achieve balance, so you control your desires—not the other way around.

Enter into a meditative state, and call in your spirit guides. Ask them to help you identify your desire. Use the following list as a reminder.

The desire for Safety: The need for stability or certainty

The desire for Wealth: An obsession with accumulating money

The desire for Education: Accumulating knowledge without purpose

The desire for Glamour: Wanting a life that's out of the ordinary

The desire for Attraction: An obsession with youth or physical appearance

The desire for Status: Wanting others to look up to you

The desire for Health: Being fixated with your physical body

The desire for Power: The need to have control over others

The desire for Fame: Craving recognition

The desire for Immortality: Wishing to be remembered after your death

Desires for:_____

Once you've identified your desire or desires, here's a way to achieve balance and ensure that they keep themselves in proportion and don't get in the way of your life plan.

Once again, enter a meditative state (see page 14) and call in your spirit guides. Ask them to support you in balancing your desire. Repeat the following:

"I call upon my spirit guides, acting in my highest interest, to help me balance my desire for _____ *and allow me to live the life my soul intended."*

When you've finished, thank your spirit guides and tell them, "Session over." Do this once a day until you feel your desire is no longer interfering negatively in your life.

Your soul wants you to create equilibrium between your physical self and your spiritual self. Glamour, for instance, doesn't exist in the Soul World. It can only be experienced here. That's why it's something your soul is eager to explore.

Your soul doesn't want to take away the fun things in life. It just wants to make sure you don't overindulge.

When Heather adopted a healthier lifestyle, did she put her desire for Glamour behind her? The answer is no. What she did was to get it to a place where it no longer ruled her life. She told me she still enjoys getting dressed up and sipping fancy cocktails with the girls. In fact, now that she's got her desire in perspective, she finds it more enjoyable than ever.

And, without the old distractions, she's able to live her life with conviction—knowing the difference between what's important and what's simply a false goal.

• • •

Now that we've explored one of the major distractions on the journey to enlightenment, it's time to walk through the Door to Transformation and discover how to overcome some of the biggest stumbling blocks you're going to encounter on the road ahead.

7: THE DOOR TO TRANSFORMATION
Challenges: Overcoming the Enemy Within

Challenges are not difficulties to be endured, but obstacles to be overcome. By destroying them, you will be less in thrall to fear and more open to your soul's guidance.

—THE AUTHOR'S CAUSAL GUIDES

A Challenge is not your friend. It gets in the way of your soul's progress and prevents you from fully manifesting yourself. Challenges are, however, a marvelous opportunity for growth. That's because overcoming them is a way of letting your soul—your true self—come shining through.

You can develop a challenge at any time, but they typically begin in childhood. Once you've got one, it may take a lifetime to overcome. (Or it may never be dealt with, and have to be worked on in another lifetime.) And sometimes, just as you feel you've beaten one, another pops up, like an endless game of Whack-A-Mole™. To make matters worse, you almost always have two of them to manage at once.

Some challenges are so mild they're barely noticeable. Others are so strong they give someone the characteristic we most associate with them. W. C. Fields was practically a caricature of someone with a challenge of Cynicism.

We adopt a challenge as a way of avoiding certain fears. In the next section, we'll examine the source of each challenge.

Cast-Iron Life Preservers

We often cling to our challenges as if our survival depends on them. Like cast-iron life preservers, they may look like they're helping us. But if we don't learn to let go, they'll slowly drag us down.

Each of us has a primary and a secondary challenge. Though they operate perfectly well independently, they'll often play off each other. Take Obstinacy, for example. It's one of the most common challenges. If it's paired with, say, a challenge of Insecurity, you might be lacking in confidence and highly resistant to change. But if it's combined with a challenge of Self-Destruction, you might be stubbornly determined to drink yourself to death.

The good news, however, is that challenges can be overcome. The way to do this is to develop the advantage and avoid the risk. With a challenge of Restlessness, this would mean learning acceptance (the advantage), and being in the moment, as a way of shaking off the risk, which is impatience.

The exercise at the end of this chapter will show how to get the better of any challenge.

The Ten Challenges

- The challenge of Obstinacy
- The challenge of Restlessness
- The challenge of Self-Sacrifice
- The challenge of Self-Destruction
- The challenge of Insatiability
- The challenge of Insecurity
- The challenge of Conceit
- The challenge of Inertia

- The challenge of Cynicism
- The challenge of Aggression

The Challenge of Obstinacy

Advantage: Flexibility
Risk: Immutability

A challenge of Obstinacy will lock you into beliefs about yourself and the world that tend not to change, even when new information comes along. It can prevent you learning new things because of your resistance to updating old beliefs.

The underlying fear is one of change. Divorced parents, relocation, and lack of emotional security are the most common childhood causes.

The inability to change can act as a block to forgiveness, because it prevents the individual from reevaluating a situation from the past. And it can make a person extremely stubborn.

The Definition of Insanity

Benjamin Franklin's quote, "The definition of insanity is doing the same thing over and over and expecting different results," might be referring to someone with the challenge of Obstinacy.

Many people stay in relationships or jobs longer than they should because of their obstinacy. Their feeling is one of "I've stuck it out this long, I'm not going to give up now."

When I saw Bridget had a very pronounced challenge of Obstinacy, I knew we were in for a bumpy ride.

Sure enough, toward the end of the session we hit a spot of turbulence. When my guides brought up the subject of her obstinacy, she denied she had any kind of problem. They began asking leading questions about how it affected her, but she still wouldn't accept it.

I thought that was it, but my guides wouldn't give up. (And neither would she!)

After twenty minutes of going back and forth, I joked, "Why don't I step outside and leave you guys to it!"

Then my guides asked her, "How do you feel about your step-mother?"

"I love her," she said.

"Are you sure?"

"Absolutely."

"Are you quite certain?"

"Yes, of course."

There was a pause, then my guides started up again. "Did you always love her?"

"No, when I first met her I hated her."

"Didn't you love her a little?"

"No, I hated her."

"Without question?"

"Yes."

"So, your belief then was that you hated her, and your belief now is that you love her."

"Yes."

And what was the point of all this? It was to get her to understand that how you see the world is not carved in stone. It can change.

My guides wanted to shake up Bridget's beliefs. It turned out that her soul wanted her to have a baby! And what was preventing her from embracing the idea was her challenge of Obstinacy. "I love my life the way it is," she said. "I'm not sure I want it to be any different."

I spoke to her a few months later. She said she'd really noticed a huge shift since our session. And what about starting a family? "We're thinking about it," she said.

The Challenge of Restlessness

Advantage: Acceptance
Risk: Impatience

Have you ever known someone who feels that everything will be fine just as soon as they find a new job, get their master's, meet the right person, move to a new city, paint the house, have a baby, retire, or reach any one of hundreds of other goals? Chances are, they have a challenge of Restlessness.

In fact, you might even have it yourself.

Enjoying the Gorilla

When my son was four years old, I took him to the zoo. All morning he'd babbled nonstop about the various animals he wanted to see. Once we got there, however, he ran from cage to cage, barely stopping to look at anything. At one point, he raced off and I caught up with him in the primate house.

I picked him up so he could see better, and said softly, "You know, instead of always thinking about what's next, you should learn to enjoy the moment."

He said, "It's not a moment, Daddy, it's a gorilla."

It's important for anyone with a challenge of Restlessness to stop occasionally and enjoy the gorilla.

What most people with Restlessness have in common is difficulty simply being in the moment. They're continually looking around the next corner.

The underlying fear is one of boredom. It can keep some of its sufferers in a constant state of activity. The cause for a lot of people is having been forced, as children, to endure long, dull hours in a classroom.

Caroline is a schoolteacher whose challenge of Restlessness made it hard for her to sit through the entire session with me.

She toyed constantly with her wedding ring, and stammered in a self-defeating race to get her words out.

I told her a story I hoped would illustrate some of the difficulties facing someone with this challenge. I said, "Sometimes it can cause extreme impatience. As a matter of fact, one of my clients who has this challenge can't even have a conversation without trying to speed it along . . . "

"Yes, yes," Caroline said, "But can we please talk about me."

I said, "We are."

Caroline told me how she can rarely sit still long enough to eat a proper meal in the middle of the day. And how she drives like a maniac, frustrated by all the "Sunday drivers" on the road.

Then she said something that summed up the challenge of Restlessness. "Wherever I am, I feel I need to be somewhere else."

As soon as the hour was up, she jumped to her feet, thanking me as she headed for the door. I said, "Do you have a class to get to?"

"No," she said, "I have the rest of the day off."

If Restlessness is your challenge, you may experience everything from mild feelings of agitation when you're stuck in traffic to an inability to sit still long enough to watch a movie or read a book.

The Need to Reflect

Educator Robert Sinclair once said, "We don't learn anything from our experience. We only learn from reflecting on our experience."

For those with a challenge of Restlessness, this couldn't be more true. That's why they complain, for example, that their kids have grown up, and it all seemed to happen in the blink of an eye.

This is not limited to those with a challenge of Restlessness. It happens to very busy people, too. So if you've ever had the feeling that your life is like a runaway train, the following technique will help you.

The solution is this: once a week, enter a meditative state. But instead of switching off your mind, reflect on everything that's happened in the last seven days. Keep a journal, and refer to it as an aid to your memory.

This will allow you to be more in the moment by processing your life as you go along.

The cure for a challenge of Restlessness is to learn acceptance: to allow life to unfold at its own pace, and to focus on the journey and not just the goal.

The Challenge of Self-Sacrifice

Advantage: Self-Determination
Risk: Martyrdom

If you grow up feeling unappreciated, you're at risk of developing a fear of worthlessness and its related challenge of Self-Sacrifice. Why? Because the way to gain appreciation is to put everyone's needs ahead of your own—to the point where your own needs don't get met.

That's not actually the best way to gain appreciation, of course. But don't tell that to someone with this challenge.

In extreme cases, these self-sacrificing souls literally work till they drop. That's such a big problem for Japanese executives that they actually have a name for it: *karoshi*. People who do this are not working hard because they need the money, but to show that they put the company or the job above themselves.

It's a grim way of seeking others' respect.

Self-pity is a common symptom of the challenge of Self-Sacrifice, as are what might be called a victim mentality and a need to suffer.

On a more mundane level, you see a challenge of Self-Sacrifice in downtrodden individuals who feel they're the victims of circumstance, or those who are always blaming other people for their problems.

Self-Sacrifice is hard on those who have it, but it can be even harder on those around them.

Last Christmas for Pam was just like it always is: an otherwise happy day marred by her mother's challenge of Self-Sacrifice.

Before Pam even sat down in my office, she announced, "That's the last time I go home for the holidays. I've had it with my mom. She drives me nuts."

I asked her to elaborate.

"My mother has practically made a career out of being a martyr. Since we were kids, she's always walked around in shabby clothes, telling everyone she's only just getting by. And she goes for free lunches at the church where they all think she's too poor to buy food. It's ridiculous! We're not rich but we're certainly not poor."

"She has a challenge of Self-Sacrifice. She wants people to see her suffer," I told her.

"She acts like life's treated her badly—but I think she does it for sympathy."

I told Pam I thought she'd hit the nail on the head. Her mom is trying to get attention by making a martyr of herself.

"So, what happened at Christmas?"

Pam took a deep breath and let out a long sigh. "Well, first of all, she told us not to buy presents for her because she couldn't afford to buy us anything. Then she brought out big expensive gifts for everyone, and sat there with nothing, pretending to choke back tears. I can still hear her tiny voice saying, 'It's all right, I don't need anything.' Aaaagh! She's such a fraud!"

And how was the rest of the day?

"It went steadily downhill. She spent the day cooking. Then, when she served the meal, she put a single slice of ham on her plate and said she was too tired to eat.

"That's when I lost it. I called her a big phony. Then my sister started yelling at me, saying that Mom's a saint. And my brother, who agrees with me, started shouting at her, and then my mom burst into tears and ran upstairs and locked herself in the bathroom . . . It was awful.

"Still," she said, with a hint of a smile, "It was better than Thanksgiving."

If you have a challenge of Self-Sacrifice, it's a sure sign you didn't get sufficient attention as a child. For this reason, it's most commonly seen in Performer types who rarely get all the attention they crave, and explains why melodrama and martyrdom so often go hand in hand.

The cure is to develop self-determination, the advantage, to allow you to take control of your destiny. The problem is that many people with this challenge would rather curse the darkness—by sticking to the risk, martyrdom—than light a candle.

The Challenge of Self-Destruction

Advantage: Self-Respect
Risk: Disintegration

Self-Destruction is the hardest challenge to overcome. The reason is that to deal with any challenge, you have to want to change. Unfortunately, those with Self-Destruction are highly resistant: if you or someone you love has ever struggled with alcohol or substance abuse, you'll understand what I mean.

A challenge of Self-Destruction can be obvious to everyone but the person who's dealing with it. Friends and family may be saying, "You have a problem," but when someone's caught up in self-destructive behavior the response is likely to be an emphatic, "I'm fine, I can quit anytime I want," or, "Keep your nose out of my business."

The source is almost always from childhood, and is caused by such traumas as abandonment, loss, a death in the family, or the feeling of not getting enough love.

Life is tough, and many with a challenge of Self-Destruction are highly sensitive people trying to cope with deep emotional pain. Remember, no one drinks themselves into oblivion every night because they're happy. What the person with this challenge is trying to avoid is reality, which is one of the reasons they so often want to alter their consciousness.

Brenda wanted to know what she could do for her son, Anthony. He was living in her basement—jobless, depressed, and doing heavy-duty drugs.

My spirit guides made one important suggestion: "Offer Anthony unconditional love."

It was clear that he had a serious challenge of Self-Destruction, and they weren't offering any reason for cheer. Like many people who have this challenge, he didn't want anyone's help. If he was lucky, he might hit bottom and turn his life around.

Sadly, he never got the chance. A few months later, Brenda came home to find him dead from an overdose.

Anthony was a sensitive Spiritualist type who was overwhelmed by life. When he was younger, he'd shown signs of depression, and had once threatened to kill himself, but it was after his father died and he lost his girlfriend (he was wearing her ring when Brenda found him) that the challenge really kicked in.

"I knew he was depressed," Brenda said, "but he wouldn't see a counselor. There was nothing I could do to help. He started using drugs, and then he was arrested. There was no probable cause, but they found packs of drugs and a gun on him."

While he waited for the trial, the prospect of imprisonment terrified Anthony, and he talked about killing himself rather than going to jail. "I really wish they'd sent him to rehab instead of letting him out on bail," she said.

"He was promised a job, but he called up in tears after the interview. He didn't get it because of the mess he was in. At the same time, my dad was dying. I had to leave home to be with him, but felt I should have stayed to keep an eye on Anthony.

"When I came back, I finally got him to go to the interventionist with me, but he was really mad about it. A few days later, he was dead."

Like a lot of people in this kind of situation, Brenda worries about whether or not she did the right thing—whether she could have done more for him.

She wanted to know if Anthony had deliberately overdosed. I asked my guides to have him talk to me directly. He was grateful for the opportunity. He'd never intended to kill himself, and wanted to express how sad he felt about hurting those he'd left behind.

My guides asked me to stress that there was no need for guilt, and there was nothing Brenda could have done to prevent Anthony's death. The challenge of Self-Destruction requires change to come from within.

The reason so many people have to hit rock bottom before turning things around is that genuine recognition of their danger only happens when they reach a nadir, their lowest point, and the very survival of their physical body is brought into question.

Sadly, for Anthony, he never got the chance.

Emotions run deep, and a person with a challenge of Self-Destruction has a fear that they have no bottom. They often cover their emotions with a blanket of bravado, pretending they're doing fine, when really they're just getting by.

Those with a challenge of Self-Destruction want to avoid reality and the attendant risk of encountering unlimited emotional pain. But when they avoid reality, a loss of identity takes place. The cure is to accept their emotional selves. The result will be self-respect, the advantage. Once self-respect is in place, the pain can be released, along with the risk: disintegration.

The Challenge of Insatiability

Advantage: Balance

Risk: Unfulfillment

Many people have a challenge of Insatiability. There are so many different ways this challenge manifests that you might not imagine they're related. I've seen it in compulsive pot-smokers, spendthrifts, and even people who have become obsessive about sports.

The root cause of this challenge is insecurity in childhood. The fear is one of loss, insufficiency, or denial.

The following story illustrates how one such childhood made a lifelong impact.

Edward is probably the richest man I know. He has property, stocks, money in the bank, and a home full of priceless antiques. Yet he can't bring himself to spend money. He won't buy a coffee when he's out because he can make one when he gets home for a fraction of what it will cost him at Starbucks. His fear of spending money has lost him friends and relationships.

When I told him the cause was a 'challenge that stemmed from his childhood, Edward knew exactly what I was getting at.

"I grew up during the height of cold war paranoia," he said. "At school, we used to practice duck and cover, where we were taught to hide under our desks in the event an atomic bomb was dropped on us. No one took it too seriously except for me. I was really freaked out. I thought nuclear war—the end of everything—was just around the corner.

"Then when I was about ten, I was rooting about in the hall closet when I found emergency rations. That really scared me. What were they for? I asked my mother but she dismissed it, saying they were in case we went camping or if there was a power failure or something.

"I didn't believe her. I thought that not only was nuclear war a possibility, but it was such a dreadful possibility she couldn't even admit it. I thought the truth must be so terrible she was trying to protect me."

Now in his late fifties, Edward still worries that a catastrophe of some kind will cause him to lose everything—so he hoards money and possessions to cushion the impact.

The cure for a challenge of Insatiability is to develop a sense of balance in your life. It's important to learn that you have everything you need in your life right now, and that your fear that it may all be taken away is unfounded.

The Challenge of Insecurity

Advantage: Self-Confidence
Risk: Unworthiness

Few things prevent you from being yourself more than a challenge of Insecurity. It acts as a barrier to fulfilling your life plan.

The fear stems from a belief that you're unworthy, and beliefs, as we saw earlier, can be very hard to change.

Insecurity is the most common challenge. As a result, few people get through life without feeling its effect. Most individuals with this challenge have suffered some kind of emotional instability in their life. If love is conditional upon certain behavior, or if Mom or Dad is kind and loving one minute but withdraws love the next, then the child will lose the feeling of security.

Should the challenge begin later in life, losing a relationship—or being in one that's not stable—is usually the cause.

Rhonda is a tall, strikingly attractive woman in her mid-twenties. She came to see me after the death of her boyfriend, a young man who'd spent years battling a challenge of Self-Destruction that had finally won out.

You'd never guess from her appearance that she had a serious challenge of Insecurity. When it came up during our session, I asked her to gauge her level of self-confidence on a scale of one to ten. She thought for a few seconds, and lowered her head. "Zero," she whispered.

Since challenges so often begin in childhood, I asked her if she could put her finger on the cause. She had no doubts. "My mother suffers from borderline personality disorder. She was unable to bond with me or anyone else. I pretty much grew up without her love."

I asked her what things were like now. She said, "My sister doesn't have anything to do with Mom anymore. It's her way of avoiding disappointment. I've stuck it out by having no expectations of her whatsoever."

For many people, a challenge of Insecurity can drag on for a very long time, preventing them from living the life their soul intended. They don't apply for jobs because "I'll never get it," or they settle for second best in a relationship since he or she is "probably the best I can hope for."

The cure for a challenge of Insecurity is to develop the advantage: self-confidence. There will be a technique for doing just that at the end of this chapter.

The Challenge of Conceit

Advantage: Humility
Risk: Arrogance

Those with a challenge of Conceit mask their true selves with a veneer of bravado. The fear is exposure: that people might see the person they really are.

The source is most often from childhood, and usually results from not having received enough attention. It can also arise from being hurt and learning to fear your own vulnerability.

Marilyn is a real estate agent in Maine. When we spoke, she seemed outgoing and confident, to the point of appearing almost arrogant. Without being prompted, she began telling me about some big award she'd won.

When I told Marilyn she had a challenge of Conceit, she didn't seem at all surprised. "I can see that," she said. There was a pause, then she added, "But I need it for my work."

My spirit guides disagreed. They pointed out that the benefits of living the life your soul intended are enormous, but can't be done if you cling to a part of your personality that isn't really you.

Marilyn had been adopted by older parents who already had several children. As she grew up, she was quiet and reserved and hardly ever spoke. As a result, she generally went unnoticed.

Things weren't helped when she was left behind at a gas station on a family trip. "I didn't think they were ever coming back," she said.

Then, when she was fifteen, the family moved, and she went to a new school where she had problems fitting in. To mask her fears, she decided to change her personality. "I became loud, brash, and a real smartass," she said.

Marilyn laughed when she looked back at how radical the change was. "One day my sister saw me near our school, being all noisy and showoffy in front of the other girls. I remember I was acting out a scene from the film *Grease*. Anyway, she ran home and told my parents—and they didn't believe her! When I came home and slipped into my quiet mouse routine, she was totally confused. She took me aside and said, 'That was really you, wasn't it?'"

It's hard to imagine that those with the most arrogance are actually among the most reluctant to reveal themselves. The cure for a challenge of Conceit is to develop humility, which will help create balance.

The Challenge of Inertia
Advantage: Self-Actualization
Risk: Stagnation

A challenge of Inertia has its roots in a fear of disappointment, and can actually appear as a fear of success.

Instead of risking being disappointed by unforeseen events, it's far easier to maintain the status quo. People with this challenge would rather stick with a boring job or avoid relationships than have to put themselves out into the world and risk being disappointed.

The source is not living up to your own or others' expectations. If Mom and Dad had their hearts set on you being a brain surgeon and you just happened to be a D student, then you might develop a chronic case of what's-the-point-itis.

If you don't apply for a job because "I'll only get rejected," you're right. You're setting yourself up for disappointment—it's a self-fulfilling prophecy.

And if you're an adult who has a string of disappointments, each knock might make you work harder to overcome your difficulties. But if the challenge of Inertia gets its claws into you, you might lose the will to fight.

Kathleen lost her will to fight soon after she left school. "Nothing," she said sadly, "seemed to satisfy my parents—particularly my dad. He wanted me to go to Harvard. I ended up at a college nobody ever heard of. He wanted me to marry a doctor and have kids, but I turned out to prefer my own gender.

"I never saw the point in working hard if I wasn't going to please anyone. God knows why my dad's approval was so important to me, but it was."

After dropping out of college, Kathleen lost all motivation. She spent two decades in dead-end jobs, dating "the first people that came along." It wasn't until she discovered gardening that she finally had something she could get passionate about. That was when she moved to a small town, met her soulmate, settled down, and started a business.

It took Kathleen years to become comfortable with being who she is. She reckoned it wasn't until her father died that she finally managed to get through a day without worrying that he might disapprove of something she was doing.

The cure for Kathleen's challenge of Inertia was to learn to live her own life through the advantage associated with this challenge: self-actualization.

The Challenge of Cynicism

Advantage: Self-Acceptance
Risk: Pessimism

Isn't a little healthy cynicism good for you? Well, yes. But not if it interferes with your ability to experience the simple joys in life.

Again, like many challenges, the source of this particular one is most often found in childhood. If you have a child who likes to act or be thought of as more grown-up than he or she is, then you may have one with a challenge of Cynicism in the making.

If you have this challenge yourself, your fear is of being thought unworldly or unsophisticated. To mask your true self, you act like you've been around the block a few times—even if you haven't.

The person with a challenge of Cynicism believes they're more sophisticated than all their guileless fellow humans. They may describe themselves as skeptics rather than cynics, but there is a big difference between the two.

"Start every day with a smile and get it over with."
—W.C. FIELDS

"Christmas? Bah, humbug!"
—EBENEZER SCROOGE

"If all the girls who attended the Yale prom were laid end to end, I wouldn't be a bit surprised."
—DOROTHY PARKER

"Deceiving others. That is what the world calls a romance."
—OSCAR WILDE

"Love: a temporary insanity, curable by marriage."
—AMBROSE BIERCE

"I was married by a judge. I should have asked for a jury."
—GROUCHO MARX

As you can see, cynicism can be amusing, but once a challenge of Cynicism sets in, it can be hard to shift. It leads to pessimism and the inability to enjoy life's pleasures. Self-acceptance is the cure, since cynics are afraid to reveal their true selves.

You might notice that I haven't used a client as an example. There is a simple reason: cynics don't generally visit psychics.

The Challenge of Aggression

Advantage: Gentleness

Risk: Belligerence

Some people believe that if you beat a child, you'll teach him respect. Unfortunately, what you're much more likely to do is create someone who will grow up to be an adult with a challenge of Aggression.

In this case, the underlying fear is one of weakness. The challenge is designed to create a self-assertive mask. What a person with this challenge is really saying is, "I've been scared in the past, and now, by acting more aggressively, I'm going to pretend I'm not afraid."

A child who's had his or her weakness exposed will adopt an air of toughness—especially in a society where physical weakness is often interpreted as a character defect.

So what's the problem? It's a tough world. Don't we need to be strong? Sure. But the big issue is this: aggression, like all challenges, is fear-based. It is, in fact, a form of weakness.

People with a challenge of Aggression start fights. And not just street fights, but major wars.

World leaders are, as I probably don't have to remind you, human too. Many of them have a challenge of Aggression. And someone with this challenge won't back down, as that would "show weakness." So when it comes to kings, presidents, and generals, history shows them rushing into wars, and staying there when common sense should tell them to cut their losses and get out. All because they don't want to appear weak.

On a more mundane level, this fear of weakness creates misery the world over, especially for children and adolescents. Bullies are almost all afraid of their own vulnerability. Not surprisingly, many bullies develop a challenge of Aggression after being bullied themselves.

The cure for a challenge of Aggression is to develop the advantage, gentleness, which is often a lot easier said than done. For many people, it's easier to stick with the risk, belligerence, than initiate such radical change.

. . .

Some of us have challenges that are barely noticeable. Others are not so lucky. Does your soul want you to simply learn to live with these issues? Certainly not. They're called challenges for a reason. According to my dictionary, the definition reads like this: "Challenge—*n.* an invitation or dare to participate in a contest."

Overcoming Your Challenges

Are you ready to do battle? The answer, if you want to live the life your soul intended, should be yes. Since challenges are blocks to growth, and overcoming them is an essential step toward enlightenment, they're to be ignored at your peril.

Here are the steps you need to take to begin dealing with them:

Step 1: Identify Your Challenges

The following statements will help you determine which are your challenges. Enter a meditative state and call in your spirit guides. Ask them to support you as you carry out this exercise.

Use the following list to remind you how each challenge manifests itself. Select the two that you can most relate to. The strongest is your primary challenge. The other is your secondary challenge.

The challenge of Obstinacy: Resistance to change; fixed beliefs; stubbornness

The challenge of Restlessness: Inability to be in the moment; impatience; difficulty "switching-off"

The challenge of Self-Sacrifice: The need to be seen to suffer; putting others ahead of yourself; self-pity

The challenge of Self-Destruction: Substance abuse; self-harm; carelessness about personal safety

The challenge of Insatiability: Immoderation; fear of loss, denial, or scarcity; greed

The challenge of Insecurity: Low self-confidence; lack of self-worth; sense of inferiority

The challenge of Conceit: Bluster; arrogance; a reluctance to reveal your true self

The challenge of Inertia: Belief that things will go wrong; reluctance to make an effort; settling for second-best

The challenge of Cynicism: Sarcastic humor; pessimism; feeling more sophisticated than the average person

The challenge of Aggression: A tendency to react aggressively; fear of appearing weak; refusal to back down

Primary Challenge:_____

Secondary Challenge:_____

Step 2: Administer the Antidote

The antidote is what you need to invoke in order to help overcome the effects of your challenge. The antidotes are listed here:

Challenge	Antidote
Obstinacy	Flexibility
Restlessness	Acceptance
Self-Sacrifice	Self-Determination
Self-Destruction	Self-Respect
Insatiability	Balance
Insecurity	Self-Confidence
Conceit	Humility
Inertia	Self-Actualization
Cynicism	Self-Acceptance
Aggression	Gentleness

Once again, enter a meditative state (see page 14) and call in your spirit guides. Ask them to support you as you administer the antidote. Repeat the following:

"I call upon my spirit guides, acting in my highest interest, to help me overcome my challenge of_____.

I ask for_____

[the antidote] to allow me to live the life my soul intended."

When you've finished, thank your spirit guides and tell them, "Session over."

$\bullet \ \bullet \ \bullet$

Challenges are some of the most serious obstructions you'll encounter on the road to enlightenment. By dealing with them, you'll be taking courageous steps toward living the life your soul intended.

Whatever obstacle you choose to confront, your soul will be behind you 100 percent, because keeping you on your life plan is something it thinks about all the time. Nudging and urging, it continually tries to prevent you from falling into the many traps that lie in wait along the path to enlightenment.

In the next chapter, we'll investigate a major way the soul takes what can seem like insurmountable hurdles and turns them into opportunities to accelerate its evolutionary process.

8: THE DOOR TO WISDOM
Investigations: Understanding Through Experience

Investigations are the soul's way of developing self-empowerment to overcome the effects of negative experiences.

—THE AUTHOR'S CAUSAL GUIDES

Emma crept softly into my office and sat down in a corner of the sofa, trying not to take up too much space. In a small voice, she told me that all was not well at home.

My spirit guides agreed. Things were, in fact, appalling. They told me her husband was physically and verbally abusive toward her.

"You're being abused by your husband," I said. "And my guides are telling me there is no love left between you. What are you still doing with him?"

"I don't know," she whispered. "I'd leave him, but I'm afraid to."

"You think he might get violent?" I asked.

"Oh, no," she said. "What I mean is I feel I'm meant to stay with him."

"Meant to?"

"It's what I'm supposed to do."

It took a moment for me to realize what was worrying her. She thought that by leaving him she'd be interfering with some cosmic plan. She'd convinced herself that some higher power wanted her to stay in this miserable marriage for the spiritual growth it would offer her.

. I explained that being abused is not the path to spiritual growth. In fact, staying in a relationship like this might be described as the path to spiritual stagnation. Her soul would never want that to happen. As it turned out, her soul was, as my guides often put it, "crying out" for her to leave. Unfortunately, she was locked in a pattern where she saw herself as the victim of a situation she couldn't escape.

• • •

The Door to Wisdom opens to reveal a source of knowledge the Soul World calls Investigations.

The harsh reality the soul has to face when it comes to the Physical Plane is that every life, however privileged, will have its share of grief, hardship, and pain. And, of course, everyone must have a soul.

When your soul looks at its approaching incarnation from the Astral Plane, it sees that certain unpleasant experiences will be virtually inevitable. Take sexual abuse, for example.

Let's say that in the upcoming life, you're the fifth child in a home where the father has sexually abused each of the other four children. And let's assume that, despite the best efforts of your soul to communicate with your father's soul in an attempt to protect you, he ends up abusing you too.

When this happens, your soul will throw you a rope in the form of an investigation—in this case, one of Abuse. It's a way of pulling you out of the worst of the quagmire.

What an investigation does is to turn even the most unpleasant experience into an opportunity for growth—one that may take decades to come to an end. It will only be completed when you learn to exert full control over it.

There is a belief that if you've suffered abuse, or any other hardship, your soul must have chosen that particular experience for a reason. That's not the case.

There is no question that your soul wants experience. And investigations offer plenty of that. But no soul seeks out an investigation for the lessons it offers. The fundamental reason is this: your soul will encounter these lessons throughout its many lifetimes without ever having to try.

What this means is that people don't suffer abuse, addiction, abandonment, or any other investigation that we'll look at, for the good of their soul, or as payback for something they did in another life.

That's why it's important to help other souls when they're in trouble—and why we shouldn't stand around suffering if we can avoid it.

The purpose of each investigation is to help you achieve self-empowerment through its advantage. Once the self-empowerment kicks in, the investigation is turned on its head. It will then become all about healing the damage. The risk is the result of the absence of self-empowerment.

The Ten Investigations

- The investigation of Servility
- The investigation of Abuse
- The investigation of Disability
- The investigation of Failure
- The investigation of Injustice
- The investigation of Loss
- The investigation of Betrayal
- The investigation of Addiction

- The investigation of Intolerance
- The investigation of Abandonment

The Investigation of Servility

Advantage: Service
Risk: Exploitation

Joan and her husband have a small restaurant in downtown Tacoma. Their relationship ran as smoothly as their business until a small change in the way tips were divided brought Joan to see me.

Joan is strong-minded and self-confident, yet she'd happily accepted a submissive role in their business relationship. That had never been a problem until now. It was all part of her investigation of Servility.

"I've worked as a waitress since we opened the place two years ago," she said. "Until a few months ago, we pocketed our own tips. Then Jim decided it would be fairer if the staff pooled their tips and divided them equally."

"That seems fair," I said.

"Fair?" she replied. "That's what I thought until we tried it. After the first night, he divided up the money, gave it to the others, and told me that I was his partner and shouldn't expect to share the staff's tips."

I suggested he might have a point.

"I'm not his partner—except in his head. There is no agreement on paper. The whole thing has been getting me down. It's like he doesn't really value me. I don't want to make a big deal about it, but it's keeping me awake at night."

My guides gave her some straightforward advice. "There is a big difference between service and slavery," they said. By treating Joan like a slave, Jim was disrespecting her. Her investigation was teaching her about being of service (the advantage) to others, but the risk was that if someone treated her without appropriate respect, she'd experience what it's like to be exploited. And that would result in disempowerment.

Joan left my office with encouragement to stand up to her husband. Just how much she did that I discovered a month later.

"I went back and told him I'd had it with being treated like a slave. I wanted my tips or a real partnership. I really laid into him. He tried arguing back, but I stood my ground."

"And what happened?" I asked.

"I got both!" she said. "He made me a proper partner and said I could share the tips too."

The Investigation of Abuse

Advantage: Resilience
Risk: Disempowerment

In certain circumstances, as we've seen, abuse may be almost impossible to avoid. When it occurs, your soul will try to protect you by detaching itself as much as possible.

That's exactly what happened to Christina.

"I was four years old when my grandfather started sexually abusing me," she told me. "And I was about twelve when it stopped. I have no recollection of that period of my childhood. I must have gone to school, had friends . . . I don't remember any of it."

Taking Refuge in the Soul World

"No soul chooses to be abused or to be an abuser. When people become abusers, they are acting against their soul's wishes. When a person is abused, he or she is not agreeing to be abused.

"When people are abused, their soul will help to minimize the damage by taking refuge in the Soul World. This can result in an out-of-body experience or detachment from the Physical Plane.

"It is the reason for repressed memories and certain personality disorders. The person who has been abused is often unaware of the incidents until their soul brings them to the conscious mind as part of the healing process."

—THE AUTHOR'S CAUSAL GUIDES

Christina's soul tried to protect her throughout that period by blocking out her conscious awareness. On a soul level, however, severe damage was done.

"I'd always blamed myself for what happened. I thought I was the one who'd done something wrong," she said.

It took many years for Christina to overcome that sense of responsibility.

"I had no innocence. The 'sexual button' was turned on when I was four—it was like I was programmed to be sexual.

"Over the years, I had many, many lovers. It was like I was seeking a sexual high, but I only ever succeeded in perpetuating the shame I felt. I got through my teens and twenties thanks to drugs and alcohol. I tell you, I've had many more years in my life I don't remember than ones I do."

Powerlessness, the risk associated with abuse, can carry over into adulthood, leading to anger and self-destructive behavior—which act as barriers to happiness.

During the first of our sessions, my spirit guides remarked that Christina was gradually learning to see men as human beings. She knew exactly what that was about. "I treated people badly—especially men. It was a way to hit back."

Christina feels that healing only happened when she found a way to deal with not just the emotional and psychological damage, but the spiritual hurt too. "To get over incest or abuse, the trick is to do it on all levels. I did it through intensive bodywork. It helped me lose the person I'd become, and reclaim the power that had been taken from me."

Fortunately, your soul will work with you to overcome damage from any abuse you might suffer in life. The first way is to turn the experience into an investigation; the second is to encourage self-empowerment, in the form of the advantage, resilience, which allows you to regain the power you lost because of the abuse.

The Investigation of Disability
Advantage: Adaptability
Risk: Helplessness

What do Einstein, Edison, the Wright brothers, Mozart, Beethoven, Mark Twain, John F. Kennedy, and Leonardo da Vinci have in common?

The answer is that they all suffered from dyslexia. And, of course, they were all extremely high achievers. That's because they didn't allow their learning disabilities to get in the way of their life plans.

The world is full of astonishing individuals whose life stories are inspiring examples of achievement in the face of great personal challenges.

Stephen Hawking wrote *A Brief History of Time,* a modern classic, despite being immobilized by motor neuron disease.

Evelyn Glennie, who hails from my little corner of Scotland, has become one of the world's most brilliant percussionists—despite being profoundly deaf.

Another great musician, Stevie Wonder, has accumulated thirty top-ten hits, twenty-two Grammy Awards, and even an Oscar for best song, despite having been blind since birth.

What these remarkable people share is a secret power: an investigation of Disability. By adopting an investigation, their souls gave each of them the opportunity to make a choice. They could give in to the seeming limitations imposed on them, or they could choose to confront those limitations by embracing the advantage: adaptability.

Lois, the elderly Spiritualist type I told you about in chapter 3, is one such person. On her first visit to me, she sat immobile in her wheelchair as my Causal guides explained the purpose of her life. We began by discussing her early years, and how she'd wanted to be a dancer before rheumatoid arthritis had forced her to change her plans.

As we spoke, I noticed something about her. Though her childhood dreams had been dashed and she'd suffered years of pain and disappointment, she showed not a sign of regret about the past.

In fact, what was astonishing was her genuine concern for everyone else in her life. If there had been a single topic for our session, it would have been "love."

Knowing she was close to death, she wanted to be reassured that everyone else was going to be all right when she was gone.

We talked for a while about each member of her family. Then she asked me about an old friend of hers. I hesitated for a moment or two when my guides gave me the answer. "Roy is dying," they told me. I knew nothing else about this person, and hated to be the bearer of such bad news. But when I told her, a look of relief spread across her face.

"Thank goodness," she said. "He's in so much pain. I don't want him to suffer any longer."

If you develop a disability that requires you to make big changes to the way you live—if you lose an arm or a leg, or if you sustain brain damage in an accident—your soul will urge you to adapt. Your soul knows no self-pity. It will be pragmatic when faced with such challenges. In fact, an absence of self-pity is a sign that you're following your soul's guidance.

Lois adapted by accepting her limitations and using her awareness of the power of love to inspire and comfort others.

In disability, we see something of the theory of evolution (which demonstrates not so much the survival of the fittest, as the survival of the most adaptable). It's why the individuals who best survive disability are those who can adapt to their condition, rather than the ones who get stuck in the purely Physical Plane response, the risk of helplessness.

The Investigation of Failure
Advantage: Perseverance
Risk: Disappointment

"This session has transformed my life," Maggie told me as she left my office. I certainly hoped so. Her life story was a litany of failures, and things couldn't have gotten much worse for her.

Over the space of two decades, Maggie had experienced more failures than most people do in a whole lifetime. She married the wrong guy, got divorced, dated another wrong guy, split up, started a business, lost it, embarked on a college course, bailed out halfway through, began another course, failed her exàms, and so on.

Try, Try, Try Again

An investigation of Failure is often found in those—like multimillionaire Milton Hershey of chocolate fame—who have had to deal with things going wrong continually.

Hershey (someone for whom, incidentally, the Illusion was virtually nonexistent) described his early years as "an unbroken string of failures." Being connected to his soul's purpose helped him use the advantage, perseverance, to keep trying until he made it.

What Maggie, a sensitive Creator type, found so transformational was discovering the reason for her failures. Throughout her life, she'd made a slew of choices more appropriate for a Hunter or Leader type. Her college courses were ones she hoped would lead to a highly paid corporate job, rather than ones that would satisfy her soul's need for creativity.

Her partners were strong, silent types whose traits were ones she, as someone who hadn't learned to accept herself, wished were her own. As it turned out, their lack of communication and inability to nurture or even appreciate her sensitivity led to the breakup of the relationships.

She was being guided to find a more sensitive partner—not a domineering father figure like the men she'd chosen before. And her soul wanted her to look for a job that would suit her Creator soul type.

For Maggie, the risk associated with this investigation—disappointment—had dogged her for years. Fortunately, perseverance, the advantage, allows someone who has experienced great setbacks to keep trying. With a clear direction to head in, she was finally ready to turn the investigation on its head.

Now she feels energized and determined to change the patterns of behavior that have been working against her. My spirit guides suggested she begin by honoring the Creator in her. She left my office asking me for directions to the nearest art store.

As Chinese philosopher Lao Tzu said, "A journey of a thousand miles begins with a single step."

The Investigation of Injustice
Advantage: Integrity
Risk: Abasement

I offered words of sympathy to a client who'd suffered severe injustice at the hands of the IRS. She shrugged her shoulders and said, "At least I'm not Leonel Herrera." It was the first time I'd heard his name, or learned of the appalling series of events that led to his execution.

Leonel Herrera was sentenced to death for the killing of two police officers. The only problem: he didn't do it. It turned out it was his brother who'd actually committed the crime.

Unfortunately, by the time the paperwork was filed, Leonel had missed the deadline for another trial. No problem, you'd think. Surely no one's going to execute an innocent man?

Leonel's case went all the way up to the Supreme Court which ruled that "actual innocence" of a crime is not sufficient reason to overturn the death penalty.

The opinion of the court was that, since Leonel's trial had gone by the book, there was nothing they could do. Justice Blackmun's dissenting opinion was that "the execution of a person who can show that he is innocent comes perilously close to simple murder."

On May 12, 1993, Leonel Herrera was executed. His last words were, "I am innocent, innocent, innocent. Make no mistake about this: I owe society nothing. Continue the struggle for human rights, helping those who are innocent . . . I am an innocent man, and something very wrong is taking place here tonight. May God bless you all. I am ready."

Like Nelson Mandela and others who have been victims of cruel injustice, Leonel achieved the advantage, integrity (how many of us would be thinking of others as we faced our own execution?), despite all that had happened to him. The risk that affects the victims of an investigation of Injustice is that they will be degraded by the experience. But this also applies to individuals who play a part in that person's investigation.

Those who could have, or should have, prevented this miscarriage of justice fall into that category.

The Investigation of Loss
Advantage: Recovery
Risk: Deprivation

"I know how people die of grief," Molly told me. "I remember sitting in a chair and thinking, 'I could sit here and never get up.'"

Molly's baby boy was born three months prematurely. For a further three anxious months, she spent eighteen hours a day in the hospital where Mark lay in intensive care. "I was there so much, everyone thought I worked there," she said.

Then, when Mark was ten months old, he died suddenly from SIDS. A medic at the day-care center tried unsuccessfully to resuscitate him.

At first, Molly was incapacitated by grief. "I was shocked at how physical it was. My arms ached to hold him. After twenty years, I still feel the love and the pain like it was yesterday. You think you can imagine what it's like to lose a child, but when it happens it's a thousand times worse."

What got Molly up from her chair and gave her the will to continue was the thought of what her death might do to her mother. "I couldn't do that to my mom. I couldn't let her feel what I was feeling."

Molly began finding ways to deal with the pain of her loss. "The first thing I did was to plant a memorial garden," she said. "Then I read everything I could. I was greatly helped by a book on death and dying by Elisabeth Kübler-Ross.

"And then someone told me about an organization called the Compassionate Friends. It took me three months to get there. The first few times, I couldn't go in. I just cried in the car for two hours. A year later, I was a facilitator and operating the emergency phone line. The same sort of thing happened when I discovered rebirthing. I ended up teaching it."

Then Molly chose to do something that would have a huge impact on her life. "I was still in shock when I made the decision to go to midwifery school. It took me a long time—to begin with I couldn't look at babies. Now, I've delivered hundreds."

Recovery is the process in which the soul heals the conscious mind by using its power to draw the individual toward the advantage. It will do all it can to help that person overcome the debilitating effects of loss.

Every person who, like Molly, has suffered profound loss will deal with their grief in a different way. Some will get caught up in the risk: deprivation, where they're unable to move beyond the feelings of loss. Molly is a self-effacing Level 10 Spiritualist with a mission of Healing, who followed her soul's guidance and embraced the advantage by helping others.

The Investigation of Betrayal
Advantage: Trust
Risk: *Uncertainty*

Howard came home and told his wife, Alison, that he'd become highly attracted to Dana, a young woman who worked in his office. Looking back, he can't believe he did it, but he asked Alison if she'd mind if he had an affair. As a Thinker type, her response was typically logical. "How can I know? I don't think I would, but until it happens I can't really say."

A week later, Howard got his answer when Alison found out he had in fact had sex with Dana.

She went ballistic.

"She was so mad, I thought she was going to kill me," he said. "She chased me out of the house with a kitchen knife."

The Betrayal of Trust

Betrayal is so common that a lot of people underestimate its potential effect. They'll try to intellectualize something that's actually happening on a profound level.

As one client said to me, "I don't know why I'm so upset. I never really trusted him." But, in fact, she did. And that's why she sued for divorce the moment she caught him with his pants down.

Relationships are based on trust. When that trust is broken, the effects can be disastrous. The shock and disappointment that results from being let down by another person can last years; the feeling of uncertainty can last a lifetime.

The investigation of Betrayal usually begins with an event, then becomes all about overcoming the risk, uncertainty, to recover the ability to rely on other people using the advantage: trust.

The Investigation of Addiction

Advantage: Autonomy
Risk: Victimization

"I'd just gotten out of jail," Carla told me. "I'd wrecked a couple of cars while I was drunk. Now they'd sent me to weekly meetings at a hospital program for alcoholics. It wasn't so bad. The meetings ended at seven, and I didn't usually start drinking till nine."

Carla is a Level 10 Thinker type whose Performer influence makes her a great storyteller. She's been sober for six years, but with a challenge of Self-Destruction, her life had to hit the skids before she turned it all around.

"All I wanted was my license back. I didn't care about anything else. I turned up at the first two meetings and lied my way through the whole thing. I pretended I was someone who just needed a little help.

"The truth was I had the walking DTs. I shook so badly I couldn't write without holding my hand down. I couldn't speak properly or formulate a full sentence. My legs were so shaky, I couldn't even keep my foot on the brake pedal at traffic lights. I'd lost my husband and most of my friends. Now, I drank myself into blackout every night.

"I turned up for the third meeting drunk. This crusty old counselor called me on it and breathalyzed me. The next thing I know, he called me a cab and kicked me out, and off the program.

"As soon as I got home, I called another cab and went straight back to the hospital. I was mad. I was working two jobs, and needed my car."

The next day, something astonishing happened when Carla went for a pizza after work with a colleague. After taking a sip out of her wine glass, it spoke to her.

"I looked at the glass and said, 'Are you the last drink I'll ever have?' And the glass said, 'Probably.' No white light; no big epiphany. But it was a real spiritual awakening. I just realized there had to be other ways to live. And whatever else it was going to be, it couldn't be scarier than the life I was living."

She turned up at an Alcoholics Anonymous meeting the next day. "I thought I might do it for six months then start drinking again. Three months later, I knew I'd never go back to my old ways."

Eventually Carla became a state rep, talking to DUI schools and Rotary clubs about AA. She still helps people in recovery. "I've made my life a living testament to the power of the program," she said.

An investigation of Addiction goes beyond being just about alcohol or drugs. It covers compulsions from sex to running. Overcoming addiction is the triumph of free will over its antithesis: victimization. Ironically, it's the abuse of the gift of free will that leads so many people to become enslaved by the object of their addiction in the first place.

The Investigation of Intolerance

Advantage: Dignity

Risk: Unworthiness

Many people, especially minorities, have to suffer the consequences of intolerance. Whole groups of individuals have experienced it in places as diverse as New York, where signs such as "No Irish Need Apply" were once common, and India, where for centuries lower-caste "untouchables" have been denied opportunities available to others.

Not being accepted for who you are can result in deep feelings of unworthiness. The investigation of Intolerance is chosen to mitigate the damage by helping you out of the risk of unworthiness. It also helps those dealing with it to achieve self-acceptance and its soul-level advantage: dignity.

Duncan is just about to leave college. He's gay, and comfortable with it. But it wasn't always so easy. He had a hard time in middle school. "I think my peers knew before me," he said. "I got a lot of verbal abuse about being gay. It was a dark time for me, but it got a little easier when we moved to another area."

He came out of the closet after he left high school. "I'd dated girls at school. They were real relationships—I wasn't covering up anything. But I realized I needed to try something else."

The big challenge for Duncan came when he told his family he was gay. His mother didn't have any problem, but his dad, who came from a very religious background, found it hard to deal with the news. "I think he hoped it was just temporary," Duncan said.

Over the last three or four years, Duncan has gained a lot of confidence in who he is. "Eventually I got to feeling that I had enough support elsewhere. If Dad didn't support me, that was his problem. I have a huge community of friends who are okay with it. I've learned to keep my head high and be proud of who I am."

And that's exactly what his soul wants him to do.

The Investigation of Abandonment
Advantage: Independence
Risk: Rejection

When Linda was a baby, her father left the family and moved to another state. She didn't hear from him again until she was fifteen, when he called her on the phone and invited her to visit him in South Carolina.

"I wasn't sure I really wanted to see him," she told me. "My grandfather had taken his place, so it wasn't like I missed out on having a father. I talked it over with my mom, and she left it up to me. I decided to go."

Things went badly from the moment he picked her up at the airport. "The first thing he said to me was, 'You're not as pretty as I thought you'd be.'

"We got in his car. There were vodka bottles rolling around the floor. He kept asking weird questions and telling me his wife could fix my hair and get me 'decent clothes.' I told him, 'You're not touching me.' Then he said he'd pay for me to go to college providing I went to Bob Jones University. It was segregated and surrounded by barbed wire in those days. I said, 'No way!'

"Then he took me on a tour of the local clubs and bars. He was constantly drinking. There was one bar—a real honky-tonk. I remember it like it was yesterday. It had the classic cocktail waitress in a Dolly Parton wig. He asked me why I couldn't look more like her. I said, 'You've got to be kidding!'

"On the way home, the car started slowing down. Finally it stopped. The next thing, he grabs me and starts tearing at my dress. He said, 'I haven't seen you naked since you were one year old.' I smacked him around and pushed him off me. He kind of sobered up a little and acted like he'd just realized what he'd done."

And that was it. Linda never saw him again.

The soul's way of dealing with abandonment is to try to control the damage by guiding the individual toward the advantage, which is independence. That's certainly what happened in Linda's case. She's one of the most independent-minded people I've met. Yet, there was no way she could avoid suffering the effects of this investigation's risk.

"No question," Linda said. "It was a case of outright rejection."

Determine Your Investigation

Some investigations are unmistakable. You might already have no doubt about yours. Others are more subtle, or may not have been around long enough to make much of an impact. Either way, your spirit guides will help you identify which investigation is currently underway in your life.

Enter into a meditative state (see page 14), and call in your spirit guides. Ask them to help you identify your investigation or investigations. Use the following reminders to assist you.

Servility: Being treated like a slave; learning to be of service
Abuse: Suffering the effects of physical, sexual, or mental abuse; developing resilience
Disability: Having a physical or mental impairment; learning to adapt

Failure: Experiencing the disappointment associated with constant failure; learning to persevere

Injustice: Suffering the degrading effects of injustice; learning to maintain integrity

Loss: Being deprived of someone or something through death or catastrophe; learning to recover from loss

Betrayal: Experiencing uncertainty as a result of another's disloyalty; learning to regain trust

Addiction: Being the victim of an addiction or compulsion; learning to develop autonomy

Intolerance: Being treated as someone of lesser worth; learning to achieve personal dignity

Abandonment: Suffering rejection by someone on whom you depend; learning to be independent

Investigation/s:_____

Once you've determined your investigation, it's time to find a way to make it work for you.

While you're still in a meditative state, call in your spirit guides. Ask them to support you in using your investigation. Repeat the following:

"I call upon my spirit guides, acting in my highest interest, to help me achieve the advantage associated with my investigation of_____ and allow me to live the life my soul intended."

When you've finished, thank your spirit guides and tell them, "Session over."

If you have no investigation currently in progress, think about someone close to you who does. You can offer them the following prayer:

"I call upon my spirit guides, acting in my highest interest, to help _____, [name] achieve the advantage

*associated with his/her investigation and allow him/her to live the life his/
her soul intended."*

As always, when you've finished, thank your spirit guides, and
tell them, "Session over."

· · ·

Each investigation is unique. No two people undergo the same
investigation in the same way. They may even be using different
investigations to explore the same experience.

Take a divorce, for example. If one partner is already on an investigation of Acceptance, his focus may be all about maintaining his
dignity and sense of self-worth.

But if the other is undergoing an investigation of Abandonment, she'll see the experience in a very different way. She may
be battling huge fears connected to her ability to survive on her
own. (Divorce for someone who's on this investigation can be
very scary.)

Investigations are the soul's way of making the best of a negative
situation over which it has little or no control. When life hands you
lemons, as they say, your soul will do its utmost to make lemonade.
It will use the advantage associated with each investigation to encourage self-empowerment.

The last thing your soul ever wants is to become a victim of circumstance. It wants you to fight back, get strong, and stand up for
yourself. Above all, it wants to prevent you from losing the ability
to live the life your soul intended.

Confronting your fears, desires, challenges, and finally your
investigations will help you to evolve spiritually by empowering
yourself. And it will propel you into the next stage of the Instruction,
which is all about creating a happier and more fulfilling future.

We're going to begin by reaching back into your soul's many past incarnations to tap into its vast wealth of experience. In this way, you'll learn to use the past to enhance the present.

PART 3: FULFILLMENT

9: THE DOOR TO CREATIVITY
Talents: Drawing on Abilities from Your Past

All talents can be used if recognized. It is important
to allow children to explore each of the talents. It is equally
important for parents to recognize that their own talents
are not necessarily those of their children.

—THE AUTHOR'S CAUSAL GUIDES

The final part of the Instruction reveals how to connect with the Soul World, and, with its support, achieve genuine enlightenment. The first step is to maximize your potential by opening the Door to Creativity, and reaching back into the past to access your natural gifts.

Decades ago, when I was a self-employed illustrator in London, I used to go through misery doing what most people would consider to be the most basic bookkeeping. Income had to be added; expenses had to be subtracted. You'd have thought it would be easy. Not for me. Numbers have always been a source of confusion and stress in my life. As a result, my books were a mess.

One day I shared the problem with a friend.

He said, "That's a nice shirt you're wearing. Did you make it yourself?"

I said, "Of course not."

"What about your hair? Did you cut it yourself?"

"Don't be crazy."

"Then why struggle with bookkeeping when you can ask some-one who's good at it to help you?"

The point is that we all have different abilities. (Bookkeeping, it turns out, is not one of mine.)

Before incarnation, your soul chooses one or more talents to help it during its time on the Physical Plane. Each one will be available to you from the time you're born until the time you die. It means that if music is one of your talents, it's never too late to learn an instrument.

Those who are most able to access their special abilities are de-scribed as talented. We act as if there is something special about them. In fact, talents are there in most people if you look for them. I was born with a talent for Intuition. Not only does it give me a natural aptitude for being psychic, but also the interest to work on it and keep developing my skills.

I've often been asked, "Don't we all have some psychic ability?"

Sure we do. And we all have the ability to play the violin. But most of us don't have the slightest interest in doing so, and fewer still have the talent.

But, if you want to play the violin and you have a talent for Music, the sky's the limit.

Talents have their origins in past-life experiences. If you're a gifted artist in this life, it means you've done it before. Perhaps you painted frescoes in Renaissance Italy. Or maybe you were once a monk who illustrated manuscripts.

Because talents create a kind of inner desire for a particular ac-tivity, having a gift and being passionate about it tend to go hand in hand.

Exploring the Talents

There are ten talents. Most of us have one or two. Some people have three or even more. Those with multiple talents are often on a mission of Exploration, where their diverse experiences may be enhanced by having access to a broader range of abilities.

Your soul will usually help bring talents to bear when opportunities come your way. Yet, it's clear that two people with the same talent can have it to a very different degree. That's because there are ways to "turbocharge" your talents—to fortify them when you particularly need them.

We'll look at ways to do that later. First let's look at the way each of the talents works.

The Ten Talents

- The talent for Healing
- The talent for Empathy
- The talent for Education
- The talent for Logic
- The talent for Art
- The talent for Communication
- The talent for Activity
- The talent for Construction
- The talent for Music
- The talent for Intuition

The Soul World regards talents as the secret behind great creativity. That may be obvious in the case of a talent for Art or Music, but it applies to every other talent as well. An accountant who has a way with figures is displaying creativity, as is a gifted acrobat or a particularly able surgeon.

The Talent for Healing

Advantage: Restoration
Risk: Sacrifice

If you have a talent for Healing, your soul will be looking for some way to use it. There is no point in bringing this into your life if it has no place to go.

I have a number of clients who are physicians. They're all accomplished healers. Yet not all of them have chosen this particular talent.

Why would someone enter a healing profession without it? One who did is the truly gifted physician I described earlier in the book. Wouldn't having a talent for Healing have taken her abilities to astronomical heights?

It might have. But there is a downside she could easily have run into: the risk of sacrifice. To be safe, her soul decided to do without it.

As my spirit guides put it, "Everything she needs to be a great healer comes from her being an old-soul Spiritualist with a Helper influence. If she'd chosen a talent for Healing, she might have sacrificed herself on the altar of medicine." (Instead, she chose a talent for Empathy, which, in recent years, has drawn her to help women who have suffered sexual abuse.)

Besides doctors, nurses, dentists, and midwives, the talent for Healing is found in many people who have chosen more alternative therapies such as acupuncture and homeopathy, and particularly hands-on healers (who also have a talent for Intuition).

But it's also a talent frequently chosen by parents, teachers, and others in order to help those in their care who have been damaged spiritually, or who are finding it hard to fulfill their potential. That's why the advantage is described as restoration. Even when a person is unaware they have this talent, they'll be motivated to help those around them complete their life plan.

The Talent for Empathy

Advantage: Understanding
Risk: Identification

Though empathy in many people is a result of the breakdown of the Illusion, the talent gives a boost to those who can generally use it in their work or in their lives.

The talent for Empathy is associated with Caregiver types and gives them the ability to understand communication that's not always verbal.

But it's not just those who are looking after children or the elderly who can use empathy. For a therapist or counselor, this talent can create a deep connection with their clients through its advantage: understanding.

Using a Talent to Enhance a Relationship

Between couples, empathy is important. Yet, like all talents, it can be ignored, unrecognized or, most often, blocked. If a person is conscious that they're not expressing empathy toward their partner, they can try accessing the talent. It's available to many more of us than you'd imagine.

Children often trigger a talent for Empathy that's been lying dormant. That's the reason many people you'd never expect to make good parents suddenly rise to the occasion when a baby is born to them.

Wendy went through her pregnancy with a sense of dread. "I thought my life was over," she said. "Everyone was so excited, except for me. I didn't want to be a mom. As I got closer to my due date, I even thought about giving the baby up for adoption."

Everything changed the moment little Elizabeth was born and Wendy's talent for Empathy popped up. "I don't think I really ever knew what love was until I saw my little girl. Now I understand why women keep having babies. It's the most wonderful thing that's ever happened to me."

Of course, as with all talents, there is a negative aspect. The risk is overidentifying with someone else. The mother who loses touch with the adult world after the birth of her baby may be crossing this line.

The Talent for Education
Advantage: Persuasion
Risk: Pontification

Every week, Tanisha had to give a report to her bosses about what was going on with their staff. The problem was that she hated having to do it. Even thinking about these meetings was making her sick.

"I'm fine with my friends, in fact everyone tells me how they can't shut me up. But once I stand up in front of a bunch of suits, the words fly out of my head," she said. "I stand there stammering and struggling to find words I've been using all my life."

We began by looking for all the usual culprits: a challenge of Insecurity, a fear of Judgment. Sure enough, there was a little of both. I showed her how to get on top of them.

Then my guides asked me to examine her talents. There it was: a talent for Education. That was why she was so good at getting her point across in smaller groups.

I showed Tanisha how to call in her talent. Now she's learning to use it to make her weekly reports less of a challenge and more of an opportunity to develop her ability in front of larger groups.

A talent for Education has the advantage of persuasion, which helps a person impart their knowledge convincingly. Its risk is pontification: imparting dogma with equal conviction.

The Talent for Logic
Advantage: Reasoning
Risk: Orthodoxy

A talent for Logic will help someone take one step at a time, and think things out in a linear way. Fictional detectives Sherlock Holmes and Hercule Poirot would agree with each other on that:

"One must rely on the little gray cells, *mon ami,* Holmes."

"Elementary, my dear Poirot. When you have excluded the impossible, whatever remains, however improbable, must be the truth."

The talent for Logic allows people to tap into their ability to think rationally in a step-by-step way—an essential qualification for scientists and mathematicians. Many of them are Thinkers who have a natural bent for this kind of reasoning anyway. But engaging the talent takes it all to another level—a bit like adding high octane fuel to the family car.

Because logic is a talent, not everyone has it. In a world where students are expected to be good at logic, the result is a lot of misery and wails of "I can't do math!"

Imagine if everyone had to be proficient in art to graduate from high school. "I can't do math!" would soon be replaced with, "I can't do art!"

Multiple Talents

The ancient Greek philosopher Socrates was renowned for his ability to argue logically. He combined a talent for Logic with talents for Communication and Education. The first helped him plan his arguments in a well-thought-out, rational way. The second gave him a facility with words. The third gave him a gift for imparting his knowledge.

A talent for Logic has the advantage of reasoning. This can be seen everywhere. Many lawyers have it, as do a lot of accountants. University professors throughout the world choose it. The risk is orthodoxy, which is why so many people in the above professions are conventional in their approach to their work.

Incidentally, many musicians also choose a talent for Logic, as it helps them see mathematical relationships between notes, intervals, chords, and scales.

The Talent for Music
Advantage: Inspiration
Risk: Technicality

Wolfgang Amadeus Mozart began composing at the age of five. Not just playing, but writing scores. As a child, he toured Europe performing his compositions on the piano, on which he was considered a virtuoso. At fourteen, he wrote his first opera.

When he died at the age of thirty-five, he left behind over six hundred compositions, including more than fifty symphonies. Needless to say, Wolfgang was a musical genius.

When his soul was on the Astral Plane planning the life it would have as Wolfgang Amadeus Mozart, it made some very careful calculations.

In several previous lives, Wolfgang had been a musician and composer. Most recently, he'd been a composer of religious music in a monastery in Sweden.

Wolfgang's soul sought out a musical family that would recognize and nurture his talents. His father was the eighteenth century's equivalent of a stage mom. His obsession with his son's career played a huge part in the success that Wolfgang enjoyed.

The Problem with Talents

Between incarnations, you choose one or more past lives that you can tap into for talents. Here's the problem: when you reach back into a past life in this way, you don't just access the good stuff, but also some of the fears and grief.

This is the reason many highly talented people are tormented, insecure, phobic, or depressive.

It's no coincidence that many great musicians were born into musical families. Imagine possessing a talent for Music, but having parents who won't encourage it, don't recognize it, or can't afford to buy you an instrument. The result could be profoundly frustrating, and it might have huge repercussions on your life plan.

The risk for many musicians is technicality, which happens when they focus on developing skill, but lose the emotion and the advantage: inspiration, which allows music to communicate with others on a soul level.

The Talent for Communication

Advantage: Expression
Risk: Digression

A talent for Communication has enhanced the lives of many people in very many arenas. Lawyers like Clarence Darrow and Johnnie Cochrane had it. Musicians like Prince and Michael Jackson have it. Performers as diverse as Maria Callas and Elvis Presley used it to connect with their audiences. Not surprisingly, the one group of people in which the talent for Communication turns up most often is actors.

What separates an actor from an actor with a talent for Communication? It's hard to describe. A very overstated Performer type like Jim Carrey has it. But so did the much more restrained James Stewart.

Walt Disney used it to help express his ideas to his staff. On one occasion, he acted out the entire story of *Snow White,* playing the part of each character to explain his vision to his animators. His performance made a lasting impression on those who went on to make the film.

Sandy is a Level 8 Thinker with Creator and Spiritualist influences. When I saw she had a talent for Communication, I said, "You've got a story to tell. Are you a writer?" She fell back in the sofa laughing.

"That's my dream," she said. "It was going to be my big question—whether I should devote myself to writing or not."

"A spiritual novel?" I asked.

Sandy let out an even louder laugh. "That's exactly what I'm working on."

An hour later, Sandy left my office, armed to the teeth with techniques for bringing her talent to bear on her work.

The positive benefit of having this talent is that it will help you express yourself. The downside is that you might slip into the risk, digression, which is often seen in highly communicative people who forget to focus on getting a clear point across.

The Talent for Construction
Advantage: Origination
Risk: Preoccupation

We all know what it's like to have a sense of satisfaction when we complete something, even if it's just cooking dinner. For those with a talent for Construction, the need to see a finished result is a major motivating factor. They want a tangible reward for their efforts.

If a child is great with Tinker Toys and Legos, that's often a sign of a talent for Construction. The same goes for any kid who's what we call "good with their hands."

When they grow up, these little Lego builders might become architects or engineers. Or they might choose occupations and hobbies where they can use their hands: guitar-making, ceramics, or building furniture. The advantage is origination, which is why they enjoy developing something from scratch.

Individuals with this talent have founded many successful companies. A business, just like a Lego project, involves planning and building, and offers concrete results.

The reward for people with this talent is seeing the fruits of their labors. Unfortunately, for many of them, having their eye so firmly on the goal keeps them locked into the risk, preoccupation, which prevents them from fully enjoying life's journey.

The Talent for Activity

Advantage: Discipline
Risk: Unrest

If you want to see this talent in action, check out Cirque de Soleil. Circus performers are often Creator or Performer types who have chosen this talent to help them on the high wire, the trapeze, and anywhere they need exceptional physical dexterity and coordination.

Take jugglers, for instance. They make great practical use of this talent and the passion it instills. Without it, few of them would ever have the patience to put up with all the practice juggling requires.

This talent brings its advantage, discipline, to great athletes too. The Olympic Games offer an opportunity for people of all soul types to express themselves. Whether it's a Thinker type competing in an archery competition, or a Creator type who's part of a synchronized swimming team, the talent for Activity will be what unites them, and what first gave them the drive to get so far in their particular activity.

A talent for Activity gives a person phenomenal coordination. Combined with the discipline, it becomes the secret power behind magicians who can make playing cards appear and disappear, or a baseball player who can connect with an incoming ball traveling at 90 mph.

Not everyone who has a talent for Activity uses it quite so dramatically. Some people choose it to help in jobs like nursing, where they'll be required to do hard physical labor.

The problem many of those with a talent for Activity slip into is the risk of unrest, where they feel they have to be on the move all the time. It can be useful for them to work out or run to let off excess energy.

The Talent for Intuition

Advantage: Insight
Risk: Hypersensitivity

Intuition is the least recognized of all the talents. Yet if you know the signs, you'll discover there are a lot more intuitive people walking around than you'd imagine.

As I mentioned in the introduction to this book, I began having psychic experiences in childhood. Like everyone with a talent, I came into the world with the ability in place—even if the Soul World had to go to extreme lengths to get my attention.

When I finally embraced my calling, I looked back on my life and saw that my past was littered with random, quite unrelated events of a psychic nature. Most were so trivial that they're hardly worth mentioning—just variations on déjà vu, or knowing what song was coming up on the radio.

One of the more noteworthy ones, however, occurred when I was a student back in Scotland. Of course, I had no idea it held the slightest spiritual significance until years later, when I started communicating with the Soul World.

It all began after my landlady's chihuahua fell in love with me. He'd swallowed a needle attached to a long piece of thread, and I managed to pull the whole thing out of his throat without hurting him. After that, he was besotted with me. We used to joke about how he thought I'd saved his life.

I had very little routine in those days. One day I might come home when classes finished, the next I might work late, hang out with friends, or play a gig with my band. Yet as long as I was home before my landlady went to bed, I'd be met with a freshly made cup of coffee.

The reason she knew I was coming was that twenty minutes before I arrived, Carlos would leap up on a stool by the bay window looking for me. We lived in a top-floor flat at the end of a crescent, which meant I only came into view at the last minute. When I did, Carlos would become hysterical with excitement.

When I walked in, he'd run around me in circles, yelping and wetting the floor (and occasionally my shoes), then I'd pet him for a couple of minutes, drink my coffee, and life would settle back to normal—until the next time.

What I didn't know then was that dogs are psychic—the result of being pack animals. In a pack, communication on a telepathic level is important. And if your dog (or even someone else's) knows when you're coming home, it's a clear sign that you yourself are psychic.

But there are other markers, too. Because time is more fluid in the Soul World, your soul will often experience emotions ahead of your conscious self. (Until I understood this, I wondered why bad news always hit me when I was already feeling down.) And since the advantage is insight, if you've seen a ghost, known about an event ahead of time, or sensed that someone was in trouble only to find out later you were right, then it's highly likely that you have the talent for Intuition.

There is, of course, a risk to being psychic—and that's hypersensitivity. Those who are psychic can find it hard not to be affected by the emotions of those around them.

The Talent for Art
Advantage: Imagination
Risk: Distraction

Creator types are the ones most usually associated with the arts. Yet anyone with a talent for Art can access it to literally create masterpieces. That's what Leonardo did.

Leonardo da Vinci was a Level 7 Thinker type with a strong Creator influence. He called upon his talent to create the *Mona Lisa,* in what has been described as his spare time. He was, after all, a Thinker, much more concerned with scientific inquiry than simply being a painter.

Creator types will often choose to get by without this talent because its risk is distraction: "I want to finish my painting, but I still haven't completed the mosaic top for my coffee table, and there is my book to illustrate . . . " And that creates distraction. It's one of the reasons Leonardo only completed a handful of paintings in his lifetime. (And why he never did finish his coffee table!)

Determine Your Talents

Enter into a meditative state, and call in your spirit guides. Ask them to help you identify which talents are available to you. Use the following list to help you:

The talent for Healing: A gift for healing; a concern for the physical, mental, emotional, or spiritual welfare of others; the ability to channel healing energy

The talent for Empathy: The ability to sense others' feelings; experiencing a connection with most people; understanding nonverbal communication

The talent for Education: A desire to impart knowledge; innate wisdom; ability to get a point across

The talent for Logic: Excellence at games like chess; mathematical skills; an analytical approach to problems

The talent for Music: An ear for music; a passion for music; the ability to play an instrument

The talent for Communication: Writing or speaking skills; expressing ideas coherently; the desire to reach out to others

The talent for Construction: The ability to plan ahead; being task-oriented; the desire to see tangible results

The talent for Activity: Enjoyment of strenuous exercise; coordination; a preference for work that involves at least some physical activity

The talent for Intuition: Psychic ability; sensing others' moods; receiving communication from non-physical sources

The talent for Art: Imagination; ability to express creativity; responding strongly to visual stimulation

Talent/s:_____

Engaging Your Talents

Now we're going to continue the exercise by bringing your talents out of your past. The method is as follows:

Enter a meditative state (see page 14) and call in your spirit guides. Ask them to support you in manifesting your talents. Repeat the following:

"I call upon my spirit guides, acting in my highest interest, to help me engage my talent. I ask for my talent for_____to be brought into my consciousness to allow me to live the life my soul intended."

Repeat this exercise for each of your talents. And, of course, when you've finished, thank your spirit guides and tell them, "Session over."

Before beginning any activity where you can make use of your talent, ask your spirit guides for their support:

"I call upon my spirit guides, acting in my highest interest, to engage my talent for_____."

Often, when I tell a client what he or she has a talent for, say, Music, they'll nod and tell me how they play the guitar or the piano, or maybe how they sing in the church choir.

Then, every so often, someone will say how they used to love playing the piano, or how they were in a band at college—all in the past tense. They'll say something like, "I used to love playing music, but I'm so busy with my job I don't have time for it anymore."

Your talents are there for a reason. Unfortunately, being so focused on our careers (another effect of the Illusion), many of us forget that what we do at work is not necessarily as important as what we do outside of work.

Whatever your talent, engaging it will give you creativity. And that will help you live the life your soul intended—one in which you're firing on all cylinders.

Having its origins in past lifetimes, creativity is truly spiritual. The more you can bring your creativity to bear on whatever you choose to do, the more you can avoid being caught up in the Illusion.

Like engaging your talents, the process of breaking down the Illusion can be turbocharged. The way to do this is to connect fully and permanently with the Soul World. In the next two chapters, we'll investigate ways to do just that.

10: THE DOOR TO SPIRITUALITY
Powers: Connecting with the Soul World

If the body is the airplane, then the conscious mind is the pilot,
the soul is ground control, and spirit guides are the emergency
rescue team. The analogy is a little simplistic, but should give
some idea of the relationship between each.

—THE AUTHOR'S CAUSAL GUIDES

The following two doors will take you to a level where you can become a being that is equal parts physical and spiritual.

The first will lead you to a place where you can make a permanent connection with the Soul World.

The second will open up to reveal the spiritual importance of reciprocity, to see others as you see yourself.

The goal is to complete the process of enlightenment.

• • •

The first step is to develop genuine spirituality.

Picture, if you will, a 1950s science fiction movie. Astronauts from planet Earth find themselves in outer space, where they meet two different alien races, living on two very different planets.

The first, the Zrogs, are surrounded by chaos and noise. Every home has at least a dozen TV sets blasting out mindless game shows. Working long hours in their jobs, the Zrogs have little time for any other recreation.

They live in isolation from each other, believing that life consists of nothing more than waking up, going to work, watching TV, and going to sleep.

The Zrogs have no interest in protecting the world they live in. They never recycle. In fact, they simply throw their trash onto the street. Their hope is that someone else will clean up the mess. Unfortunately, no one ever does.

The second, the Lanusians, are quite the opposite. They value tranquility and relaxation. To this end, they set aside plenty of time every day to meditate.

Lanusians take pride in their belief that they work to live, not the other way around.

Each Lanusian feels connected to the natural world. They recycle and avoid depleting their resources or polluting the environment. They do all they can to ensure a healthy planet for themselves and their children.

Knowing that life is not a one-off experience, they want to make certain that their next incarnation will be as pleasant as the current one.

Now, let me ask you a question:

Which of these two races is living the more spiritual existence?

A: Zrogs ❑
B: Lanusian ❑

I hope your answer is "B." (If you answered "A," I suggest you go back to page one and start this book over.) We all know instinctively that a peaceful, environmentally conscious race of aliens has to be more spiritually advanced than one that's loud and self-centered.

The reason is that, on a soul level, we all know what it means to be spiritual.

But how can spirituality be achieved? What can you do to live a spiritual life?

Spirituality happens naturally when you connect to the Soul World through your spirit guides. The good news is that connecting is not that hard to do.

It's not restricted to certain individuals. You don't have to be smarter, holier, eat a particular diet, worship a specific deity, climb a mountain, or become a hermit.

You simply have to develop superpowers.

Superpowers?

That's right. Not the kind that allow you to jump tall buildings, but ones that will connect you to the unlimited support of your spirit guides by helping you smash through the Illusion.

These powers will give you clarity and insight. They'll help you create clear destinations to aim for. And they'll allow you to call upon your spirit guides whenever you need them.

Until now, you've probably spent more time planning your Thanksgiving dinner than the course of your life. But you're about to change all that.

The more work you put into planning and preparation now, the greater your chances of ending up with the future you want—one that's in harmony with your soul's desires and your life plan.

Are you ready for this? It could change your life.

Connecting with the Universe

Your powers, once developed, will be with you for the rest of your life. As long as your motives are pure, your ability to draw on the support of your spirit guides will grow increasingly stronger with time.

In this section, we'll examine each of the ten powers and discover how to create the future you want. The advantage associated with each is what you need to achieve a spiritual connection with the Soul World. The risk is what you'll encounter by clinging to the Illusion.

The Ten Powers

- The power of Tranquility
- The power of Clarity
- The power of Relaxation
- The power of Integrity
- The power of Protection
- The power of Visualization
- The power of Intention
- The power of Communication
- The power of Guidance
- The power of Action

The Power of Tranquility
Advantage: Serenity
Risk: Distraction

In a world full of chaos, noise, and constant stimulus, it can be virtually impossible to get the tranquility your soul needs. And accessing the power of the universe requires a still mind.

The Zrogs are too distracted by the constant din that surrounds them to take even this small first step. Even here on Earth, finding a little peace and quiet can take considerable effort.

That's why the first stage in the process of manifesting the future you want is to find peace. Or, more specifically, a safe, quiet place where you won't be disturbed.

You might create a cozy corner in your living room or bedroom. One of my clients made a "nest" in a corner of her room. She bought a comfy old armchair, a small oak desk, and a green glass banker's lamp.

Twice a day, at least, she'd use this spot as a place to meditate, journal, read, or simply think. The rest of the family learned that this was her special area, and didn't interrupt her when she was there.

The Soul World has its reasons for having you find your own space. It wants to detach you from the constant noise and drama that surrounds you. By having a particular place, and even certain times that you use it, you'll create an agreement with your spirit guides that this is your special time together. And by avoiding the risk, distraction, you'll find it possible to slip into the advantage of serenity with relative ease.

The Power of Clarity
Advantage: Lucidity
Risk: Indecision

The clearer you are about what you want your future to look like, the easier it is for your guides to help. But how do you get clarity?

I know this might seem a little mundane, but the secret is to keep a journal. It's an incredibly important step toward fulfilling your life's purpose. Let me give you a computer analogy:

Your brain is the hard drive; your journal is a recordable CD. If your hard drive is full, there is no room for new information to come in. But if you dump everything you don't need onto the CD, you can free up lots of space where you need it most.

If your brain is full of shopping lists, worries, unwritten notes to yourself, and a host of other things you don't need to keep in there, transfer all that stuff to your journal. (This is an essential step toward avoiding the risk of indecision.)

Do this regularly and, though you may never run out of trivia, you'll allow more important thoughts to come through, thanks to the advantage: lucidity.

The Power of Relaxation
Advantage: Receptivity
Risk: Impregnability

Once you've created a tranquil space both within and without, it's time to begin the process of connecting to the universe.

The first step is to calm your mind. If the inside of your head looks like a Jackson Pollock painting, with random thoughts swirling around chaotically, then any direction you get from your spirit guides will get lost in the confusion.

The way to create a mind that's receptive to guidance is to meditate. (Refer, if you like, to the method described in the introduction.)

The advantage is receptivity, where you make it possible for your spirit guides to get through to you. Without opening up in this way, it's hard to avoid the risk: impregnability, where your conscious mind creates a barrier between this world and the next.

The Power of Integrity
Advantage: Support
Risk: Restriction

I had a session with a concerned grandmother. She was worried that her two grandchildren weren't being raised properly. I couldn't do a thing for her. Not only was she not the primary caregiver, but her motives were dubious. She was more concerned with showing up her daughter's failings than supporting the family. My guides cut off the conversation the moment it wandered from genuine concern to nosiness and malice.

Integrity is essential when it comes to dealing with spirit guides. Don't forget, they know everything. If you have an ulterior motive—a desire to find out how much Aunt Agatha has in her bank account, or the intention of putting a curse on your ex-boyfriend—forget it.

But if you want your guides' support in living a more purposeful life, or help raising your family, they'll be with you every inch of the way.

The secret is to question your motives at all times. If you act with integrity, you'll be rewarded with the advantage: the support of the Soul World. If you don't, you'll discover the risk: restriction, where a wall will come down between you and your spirit guides.

The Power of Protection
Advantage: Safety
Risk: Vulnerability

Before you start talking to the Soul World, there is a word or two of warning I need to impart.

Would you ever think of dialing a number at random and asking a complete stranger for advice?

Of course not.

Yet, that's what many of us do when we talk to those invisible entities on the other side.

We tend to believe that everyone on the Astral Plane is somehow kindly and benevolent. They may be "in spirit," but they're not necessarily "spiritual." Remember your drunk Uncle Harry? The one who used to put the lampshade on his head at parties and lead everyone in a conga line, singing "Hot, Hot, Hot?" He's there.

"You Are the Chosen One"

If a spirit guide presents itself as exceptionally enlightened, or full of ancient wisdom, watch out.

And if it flatters you, or tells you you're somehow special, tell it to take a hike. Genuine spirit guides never, and I repeat never, use flattery or brag about their qualifications.

Only lower Astral Plane entities behave like that, and they're not, in any sense of the word, enlightened.

Spirit guides exist on two planes. Most guides on the Astral Plane have completed all their lives on the Physical Plane. (Though some souls who are between incarnations will assist those with whom they've had a close connection while incarnate.)

Those who have reunited with their soulmates while on the upper Astral Plane will advance to the Causal Plane to become elevated spirit guides. (Spirits beyond this level can only communicate with us through intermediaries on the Causal Plane.)

A simple way to be sure you're getting your information from genuine spirit guides is to ask yourself two questions: "Does the information make sense?" and "Does it empower me?"

Communication with other planes can be dangerous. Some methods leave you wide open to being taken advantage of by malevolent spirits. I've known several people who have used a ouija board without protection, and then got upset when they were told they were going to die horribly.

All that was happening was that they were hooking up to mischievous lower Astral Plane entities.

That's what happened to Hazel. She came to see me about something that was causing her a great deal of stress. She was in her mid-fifties, but worried that she'd never see sixty. She told me how she'd begun using a ouija board several years before. One of the first questions she'd asked the spirit world was when she was going to die. They told her she'd die at exactly the age of fifty-nine. And no matter how often she asked the question, she got the same answer. She wanted to know if time was really running out.

I began by calling in my spirit guides and ensuring I was protected while I channeled.

"What are you doing?" she asked.

"I'm asking for protection and making sure I'm connected to my spirit guides," I told her.

Hazel squirmed. I smiled at her and she smiled back uncomfortably. What I said next hardly required saying.

"You just launch straight in, I suppose."

Not surprisingly, that was where the problem lay.

My spirit guides assured her that she might well die at fifty-nine. Or seventy-three, or ninety-two, or just about any time. These things are not carved in stone, and, with a few exceptions, it isn't in our interest to know when we're going to die.

Which Spirit Guides?

In my sessions, I use Causal guides for all the "big picture" questions—the ones that have to do with life plans and past lives. But if I wanted an answer to a question like "Is Grandpa happy on the other side?" I'd ask my Astral guides.

With spirit guides on both the Astral and Causal Planes, which ones should you call in? The answer is to let them choose. By simply asking for "spirit guides, acting in my highest interest," you'll let them decide who's best for you.

Protection is a way to make sure that you connect to benevolent guides, and keep drunk Uncle Harry and other troublemakers away from you while you're in a vulnerable state. The advantage to Protection is safety. The risk of not engaging this power is vulnerability.

Power of Visualization
Advantage: Direction
Risk: Aimlessness

Visualization allows you to create impressions that will help you determine where you're going and how to get there.

By visualizing your future, you and your guides are creating a destination: something to aim for. The advantage, direction, will give you a clear purpose and help you avoid the risk, aimlessness, which prevents so many people from achieving their goals.

By stilling your mind and calling in your spirit guides before you begin, you'll give them the opportunity to channel images to you. Visualization is a collaborative effort.

The technique for doing this will be given later in this chapter.

Power of Intention

Advantage: Conviction
Risk: Uncertainty

The more engaged you are in changing your life, the more your spirit guides will be too.

My guides often talk about bringing a certain desire to the front burner. If you want to be a successful artist, for example, you have a far greater chance of seeing your dreams come true if you paint every day, attend figure drawing classes in the evening, visit art galleries on the weekend, and read books on the subject at bedtime.

Similarly, if you want to meet your soulmate, there are ways to speed up the process of bringing that person into your life. And of course, it works with anything you choose.

The secret is to be clear about what you want, and to keep asking your spirit guides for their help. If you begin your meditation twice a day by saying, "I ask you to help bring my soulmate into my life. Please act upon my request," you'll both put finding a soulmate onto the front burner.

Voicing your intention repeatedly will help you develop conviction, the advantage, and help you to avoid the risk, which is uncertainty.

The Power of Communication

Advantage: Consensus

Risk: Ambiguity

When I began contacting my spirit guides, one thing that surprised me was just how much they want to talk to us. I'd always assumed we were the ones who wanted to communicate, not them. I ended one of my first ever sessions with a thank you to them. They said, "Thank you, too. You give us a purpose."

"Would You Mind Awfully Much . . . "

Talking to invisible entities on other planes takes skill and effort. My earliest attempts at asking questions taught me the importance of phrasing every question to avoid ambiguity.

My first mistake was to ask (in my polite Scottish way) questions that began with "May I ask you . . . " I wondered why I kept getting the answer "Yes," until I realized they were saying, "Yes, you may ask us . . . "

Spirit guides have to be pedantic. If they were not, communication with them would be full of inaccuracies.

And they've taught me to be pedantic too. Being specific has come in useful when I do work, like medical research, where accuracy is essential.

Way back, when I'd just started doing sessions, a client asked me to ask my guides what was causing her asthma. I couldn't get an answer. I struggled for five minutes to get a response, until I tried asking, "What's triggering Laura's breathing problem?" Suddenly they were talkative again. They came up with a list of half a dozen allergens that were causing her to wheeze, but stressed that she didn't have asthma.

It's vitally important to be specific. "Guides, I'd like you to help me become happy," is a request that causes your spirit guides to shrug their shoulders and look blankly at each other. (Not literally, of course.)

On the other hand, "Guides, I want your help in getting that job I've just interviewed for" gives them something to get their teeth into.

Ask your questions without vagueness, and you'll achieve the advantage: consensus, where you and your spirit guides agree on what it is you're trying to achieve. On the other hand, ask two questions in one, or approach your guides obtusely, and what you'll end up with will be the risk, which is ambiguity.

The Power of Guidance

Advantage: Synergy
Risk: Unilateralism

Many people expect answers from their spirit guides to come to them like a voice in their heads, but that's not generally how it works. Most often, you'll get their response in a way that's subtle, but strong.

Imagine you have two options ahead of you. Let's say you've been offered two different jobs. Job A pays better than job B, but it's in another city, meaning you'd have to relocate. Job B comes with a car and all sorts of benefits, but it means you'd have to work shifts, which is something that doesn't appeal to you. What are you going to do?

The first thing is to describe the options to your spirit guides. The second is to ask them to give you guidance. The third is to wait for an answer.

The way the answer comes is often in the form of clarity. You might be driving in your car ten minutes later, or sitting around at home the next day, when you think to yourself, "Why did I ever think job B was an option?" Suddenly the choice is clear.

The advantage associated with the power of Guidance is synergy; together, you and your guides achieve far more than either of you could have done separately. Without guidance, your risk is unilateralism, where you separate yourself from your spirit guides and have to go it alone.

The Power of Action
Advantage: Actualization
Risk: Unfulfillment

You've learned how to ask the universe to support you in achieving your goals. Now it's time to do your part.

It's up to you to recognize and seize opportunities as they come along. Your spirit guides can only do so much. They can help put a door in front of you, but only you can choose whether or not to walk through it.

So, when opportunities come along, ask yourself if they fit into your plan for the future.

Seizing Opportunities

If you visualize yourself sailing around the world in ten years' time, and someone offers you the chance to crew a yacht that is heading off to the Bahamas next week, you might recognize it as an opportunity to get closer to your goal.

Even if you're not ready for the big trip just yet, perhaps the training will come in useful, or you'll meet people who will help you in the future.

The important thing is to ask yourself whether or not it supports your vision for the future.

The advantage associated with the power of Action is actualization, where you engage fully with your life plan. The alternative, the risk, is unfulfillment, and that's something your soul wants you to avoid.

Don't forget, when you're sitting in the senior center reflecting on the life you had, it's the opportunities you didn't take, rather than the ones you did, that will be a cause for regret.

Using Your Powers

The Power of Tranquility
Sit comfortably in a quiet space where you know you won't be disturbed for at least an hour. Switch off your cell phone or other potential distractions.

The Power of Clarity
If you have particular worries or thoughts that are distracting you, write them all down in your journal before moving on to the next step.

The Power of Relaxation
Close your eyes and enter into a meditative state for at least twenty minutes, or until you feel completely calm.

The Power of Integrity

Bring in your spirit guides in the following way:

"I call upon my spirit guides, acting in my highest interest, and ask that all information I'm given is for the highest good of all concerned."

The Power of Protection

Ask for protection from mischievous Astral Plane entities:

"I ask my spirit guides to protect me from negative energy in all my communications with the Soul World."

The Power of Visualization

The next step is to visualize yourself at a point in the future.

Use the list below to make sure you explore all the different facets of your life.

- Location
- Home
- Relationships
- Career
- Recreation
- Rest
- Friendships
- Travel
- Health
- Spirituality

Begin by picturing your life ten years from now. What does it look like? Who's in it? Where are you?

Do this until images stop forming. Now visualize your life five years ahead. When you feel images are no longer forming, do the same for one year from now.

The Power of Intention

In your journal, write down ten things you saw in your visualization that you want to have in your future. These are your goals.

The Power of Communication

Engage the support of your guides in achieving your ten goals, using the following request:

"I ask for your help in bringing [list the ten goals] into my life to allow me to live the life my soul intended. Please act upon my request."

The Power of Guidance

At least once a day, make a point of asking your spirit guides for direction. Take a few minutes to listen to your guides' response. Review each of the requests you've made, and ask yourself if you're closer to achieving your goals.

The Power of Action

Begin taking steps toward living the life your soul intended. The first is to make a list of ten things you can start doing immediately to achieve the goals you created.

• • •

Your spirit guides are available to you at all times. By engaging their support, you'll develop a deep sense of inner peace. (That's one of the reasons we associate spirituality with tranquility.)

If you can get into the habit of talking to your guides at least once a day, you'll soon find that you can sense their presence around you. And if you ask for their support, it won't be long before you learn to recognize their direction.

Creating a permanent connection with your spirit guides allows you to step from this world into the next. Once you do that, something transformational will happen. You'll feel a sense of unity, not only with them, but with all the other souls on the planet.

As this feeling of connection grows, you'll discover that you've become a Lanusian! Perhaps not literally, but your heightened awareness that we are all on this journey together will help you to act like one.

It's a mark of someone who is truly spiritual to accept others. If you can remember that, you'll make a subtle but strong impact on those who are less spiritually advanced than yourself.

A Word about Acceptance

A client once asked me if accepting others meant letting someone rob you if they wanted to.

The response from my guides was emphatic: "Condoning bad behavior is not a spiritual act—it does not help anyone. Being spiritual does not mean giving others permission to act in a harmful or destructive way.

"Being spiritual means accepting that not everyone sees the world the way you do. It also means helping others to become more spiritual themselves. The way to do that is by example."

If you try to help the next Zrog you meet by pointing out your innate superiority and offering to show him the way, will he thank you? No, he'll probably zap you with a matter discombobulator.

What you can do instead is to lead by example. Rather than looking down on the Zrog, you might bear in mind that you weren't always the spiritually superior being you are now. You were once (in another lifetime, if not this) up to your eyes in the Illusion, and unable or unwilling to see the world in any other way.

By simply living your life in a more spiritual manner, you'll show those who are wrapped up in the Illusion that there are other, more productive ways to live.

Now, as we move on to the final part of the Instruction, you'll discover how to take the last few steps to completely break through the Illusion. The results will be illuminating.

11: THE DOOR TO ENLIGHTENMENT
Paths: Acting from Your Soul

Acting from your soul means following the paths at all times. It is through walking the paths that true enlightenment may be reached.
—THE AUTHOR'S CAUSAL GUIDES

What is enlightenment? It means acting in a way that's compatible with your soul's purpose. You've already done much of that by learning who you are and why you're here, and connecting with your spirit guides. But it also means behaving in a way that supports other souls. To do that, you have to integrate your Physical Plane self with your Soul World self.

That means stepping out of the darkness of the Illusion and into the light.

The Door to Enlightenment will take you on a journey along ten paths. Each one will help you get a little closer to your soul. In fact, walking the first nine will automatically take you to the tenth: the path of Love.

Following the ten paths is not as hard as you imagine. It doesn't call for you to give up your worldly possessions, separate yourself from your friends and family, or follow some sort of esoteric teaching.

All you have to do is treat others exactly as you'd have them treat you.

The Golden Rule. Simple.

Once you start following the paths, you'll find the results astonishing. It's no exaggeration to say that you can use them to recreate the world around you.

• • •

On a sunny August afternoon, Walter slowed his Aprilia Mille motorcycle as he got behind a slow-moving police officer on her Harley-Davidson.

She pulled over to the side of the road and stopped. Walter carried on past her, doing about 15 mph. The next thing he knew she was behind him, her lights flashing. He stopped and got off his bike, wondering what the heck he'd done.

"License plate obstruction!" the officer said sharply.

Walter looked at her blankly. The plates on his bike were in the same place they are on all bikes of that make and model. Nothing was hanging over them or hiding them from view.

"Where's the obstruction?" he asked her.

"License plate obstruction!" she repeated.

Walter was losing his patience. "Where's the obstruction?" he asked again. The officer refused to answer. She simply tore off a ticket and handed it to him.

Walter was flabbergasted. The whole situation seemed surreal. As she walked away, he shouted after her, "This is a disgrace! You're a disgrace! I'll see you in court—I'll have your sweet ass on a platter!"

Some weeks later, Walter turned up at the magistrate's hearing. By the time he got there, he'd had plenty of time to stew. He was still furious about the ticket. And he was mad at having to fight his way through rush-hour traffic and, being a self-employed construction worker, losing a morning's pay.

Adopting the same pose on the sofa in my office, Walter described how he slumped down in the chair opposite the magistrate. He was surly, and deliberately trying to look menacing. The magistrate was the complete opposite. She was professional and detached.

"What's this all about?" she asked.

Walter didn't say a word.

The magistrate said, "You're not talking?"

"No," he replied sarcastically.

As they stared at each other in complete silence, Walter pulled out a photograph he'd taken of the rear ends of four motorcycles. He slapped it down on the table between them.

The magistrate stared at it for a few seconds. Politely but firmly she said, "Let me guess. One of these is yours and I'm supposed to figure out which?"

Walter didn't reply. He simply nodded his head.

"Your attitude won't help you. You can pay a fine or go to court," she said.

Walter sat up. "You mean I have to come back?" he shouted.

The magistrate ignored his outburst. "I can schedule a court date. I imagine you want to?"

"You bet!"

"Do you want the police officer there?"

"Oh, yeah!"

As the magistrate passed the paperwork to her secretary and left the room, Walter let off some steam. "You people have completely wasted my time. This county has wasted my time!"

And then something hit him—a kind of awareness. In a flash, Walter realized he was being, as he put it, a "total asshole."

He said to himself, "I don't want to carry all this resentment around with me. This isn't the person I am."

He gave the secretary a big smile and said, "I'm sorry about the way I've been behaving here." Then he walked over to the magistrate's office. He knocked on the door and walked right in. She looked up from her desk with a "what is it now" look on her face.

Walter smiled and said, "I was so rude I can't believe myself. And you weren't. Thank you for being so nice to me when I wasn't to you. I'm sorry."

The magistrate looked a little surprised. "Thanks for saying that," she said.

As Walter left, he felt fantastic—as if a huge load had been lifted off his shoulders. He couldn't believe he'd allowed some stupid little issue like a ticket to get him so bent out of shape.

Out on the street, standing beside his bike, Walter zipped up his leathers. He was just about to put on his helmet when he saw the magistrate rush out of the building, obviously on her way to lunch. She glanced at him and gave him a friendly smile.

All of a sudden, she stopped. She stared at the bike for a few seconds. Walking over to it, she squinted at the license plate.

"Is this the bike?" she asked.

Walter nodded.

"I thought the exhaust pipes might be in the way," she said. "What's the problem?"

When Walter heard those words, he said, it made his day. He shrugged his shoulders. "I don't know," he said.

"This is ridiculous!" she said. "Come with me!"

Walter followed the magistrate back up to her office. She asked her secretary for his file. Taking a Sharpie, she scored a big X across the ticket.

"Case dismissed," she said firmly.

Walter gasped. "Are you kidding? Thank you so much!"

"No problem," she smiled. "Have a nice day."

Exploring the Paths

Sitting in my office, a month later, Walter told me, "That moment changed my life."

Although, superficially, this interaction between these three people—Walter, the police officer, and the magistrate—may seem mundane, it has enormous spiritual significance.

I want to show you now how Walter's story touches on each of the paths, and why it had such an impact on his life.

The Ten Paths

- The path of Cooperation
- The path of Respect
- The path of Knowledge
- The path of Equality
- The path of Understanding
- The path of Justice
- The path of Truth
- The path of Peace
- The path of Freedom
- The path of Love

The Path of Cooperation
Advantage: Reciprocity
Risk: Selfishness

Cooperation is essential to our survival as a species. The path of Cooperation helps us to learn the important benefits of reciprocity.

When Walter stepped off his motorcycle to face the police officer, he showed the desire to cooperate. When she refused to cooperate by not answering his questions, she set in motion a cascade of events that wasted a lot of time and effort for everybody concerned.

Cooperation

Overfishing has caused cod supplies to collapse. It's in everyone's interest to stop fishing to allow stocks to regenerate. Unfortunately, there are huge short-term financial reasons that make it hard to get those whose survival depends on fishing to cooperate.

Everyone may understand the consequences and agree to a moratorium. But if even one fisherman decides not to cooperate and keeps fishing, others will join in. The result is that the fish disappear and everyone goes out of business.

It's important, also, for those in power to follow the path of Cooperation and give financial incentives to encourage compliance.

Cooperation is one of the first lessons the soul is exposed to when it comes to the Physical Plane. Through learning to work together, it gradually learns that acting in the interest of others is actually in its own interest.

Those who have broken through the Illusion are the ones most likely to follow the path of Cooperation. Conversely, those who are caught up in the Illusion are the least likely to act in a way that benefits all concerned—including themselves.

The advantage of cooperation is reciprocity—where one person helping another leads to that person returning the favor. The risk is selfishness, and that happens when an individual reaps the benefits of cooperation without reciprocating.

The Path of Respect

Advantage: Dignity
Risk: Disrespect

The path of Respect takes you to a place where you can learn that another human being is no less important than yourself.

When Walter chose to see the magistrate as a fellow human being, he was able to put himself in her place. That's when he walked the path of Respect. He realized that how he'd behaved in her office was not how he'd like to be treated himself.

By taking the path of Respect, he conferred its advantage, dignity, upon her. And since all paths are reciprocal, he, in turn, dignified himself rather than slipping into the risk, which is disrespect.

The Path of Knowledge

Advantage: Awareness
Risk: Ignorance

The path of Knowledge begins with the desire to learn. It's not about being smart as much as being curious.

Once the magistrate learned the facts of the case, she used them to reassess her initial evaluation. That, of course, had been based on the opinion of the police officer and her unpleasant initial contact with Walter himself.

The path of Knowledge requires an open mind and the courage to question everything. It's often said that knowledge is power. On a spiritual level, that couldn't be more true. Knowledge creates awareness; its absence leads to ignorance and spiritual stagnation.

The Path of Equality

Advantage: Connection
Risk: Uniformity

As we walk the path of Equality, we gradually realize that we're in this life together.

When the magistrate and Walter took their short walk back to her office to take care of the ticket, he was no longer an uncouth biker, and she was no longer the frosty symbol of uncaring bureaucracy. They went as equals: two people recognizing each other as worthy of respect.

Taking the path of Equality means looking beyond rank, status, and superficial differences, and seeing one another as fellow human beings.

The path of Equality leads to connection: the awareness that we're all one. The risk is uniformity, which happens when equality is seen from a purely Illusionary perspective.

The Path of Understanding

Advantage: Forgiveness
Risk: Assumption

The path of Understanding requires the ability to put yourself in someone else's place and to appreciate their perspective.

That's exactly what both Walter and the magistrate did to each other. Walter didn't have to apologize for his boorish behavior. But when he had the sudden awareness of how badly he'd behaved, he saw how she must have seen him.

And when the magistrate saw that the license plate was perfectly visible, she felt Walter's frustration.

They both behaved as they did because each understood the other's position.

The path of Understanding has a subtle power, which can be seen in its advantage: forgiveness. When the magistrate saw how Walter had been unfairly treated, his behavior in her office made sense. And that led to her forgiving his rudeness.

Walter demonstrated the risk when he threw the photograph down on the magistrate's desk. It's one of assumption—where you seek someone's understanding without giving them sufficient information to do so.

The Path of Justice
Advantage: Fairness
Risk: Injustice

The path of Justice requires that you ask yourself, "Is it fair?"

Did the police officer ask herself that question? Probably not. If she'd been the one getting a bogus ticket, she'd have no doubt recognized the unfairness of the situation right away. As it was—and as someone in thrall to the Illusion—she got more out of exerting her power than she did out of acting from her soul.

Like all paths, the path of Justice is a two-way street. It requires the ability to both give and receive. The more fairly you treat someone, the more likely you are to experience fairness in return. For the same reason, injustice leads to injustice.

The Path of Truth

Advantage: Honesty

Risk: Mistrust

The path of Truth is where you put your integrity to the test. The reward is well worth the risk. By behaving honestly, you receive the trust of others and the support of the Soul World.

Was the police officer interested in the truth? Was she lying when she insisted that Walter's license plate was obscured? Such a thing is purely subjective. But if she'd been totally honest, wouldn't the truth have spoken for itself? Wouldn't she have been able to explain herself, instead of barking "Obscured license plate!" over and over again?

The path of Truth leads to honesty. Lies, on the other hand, create disbelief—which then turns to mistrust.

The Path of Peace

Advantage: Power

Risk: Submission

The path of Peace is the one we often forget applies to others, and not just ourselves.

When Walter faced the magistrate across her desk, when he deliberately tried to intimidate her, he acted from a place of aggression. Did he get what he wanted? Not surprisingly, no.

The magistrate had a right, as does any human being, to feel safe from aggression at all times. Faced with Walter, she protected herself by sticking to the rule book. It was only later, when Walter took to the path of Peace, that she dropped her guard and made an extra effort to help him out.

Peace is power. But achieving peace requires being proactive.

Otherwise, it loses its strength. (Submission, the risk, may look like peace, but it's actually a form of weakness.)

The Path of Freedom
Advantage: Opportunity
Risk: Recklessness

The path of Freedom means following your life plan without interference from others.

In Walter's case, freedom meant the ability to ride his bike without the risk of being apprehended by the law and fined the equivalent of a day's pay for no genuine reason.

Walking the path of Freedom means allowing one another the maximum opportunity to live our lives in the way we want—providing that right is exercised responsibly.

If Walter had been stopped doing 90 mph in a residential area, his freedom would have morphed into recklessness. Pedestrians, after all, have the same right to freedom as bikers.

The Path of Love
Advantage: Altruism
Risk: Martyrdom

The nine paths lead to the last: the path of Love. This means it's not necessary to ask yourself if you're acting out of a sense of justice, equality, fairness, and so on. You can simply ask yourself if you're acting out of love.

The path of Love takes you to altruism—the soul's highest ideal. Altruism can be described as selflessness—and that doesn't mean self-sacrifice. Martyrdom may appear selfless, but it's not; it happens when you forget that you, yourself, are as important as everyone else on the planet.

Where Does the Self-Interest Go?

At the beginning of this book, I described how the soul's journey takes it from self-interest to altruism, and I asked the question: where does the self-interest go?

The answer is that it never actually leaves. What happens is that the altruism balances the effects of self-interest, so you learn to value your interests and those of others equally.

When you walk the path of Love, you make a connection between your conscious mind and your soul.

When Walter connected with his soul, however inadvertently, he broke through the barrier of the Illusion. And that's why the event was so incredibly momentous for him.

In the magistrate's office, Walter connected fully with his spiritual self. In an instant, the Illusion evaporated and he opened up to his soul's direction. He did the right thing because the Illusion no longer got in the way.

When we discussed what happened that day, Walter couldn't emphasize strongly enough how significant the event had been.

"It was one of the single most important moments of my life—up there with my mother dying."

He described how he'd dragged anger around with him all his life. "I'd get a ticket for something trivial—seven miles an hour over the limit—and it would eat me up. This incident was like the final straw—the ultimate stupid ticket!

"But something happened at the secretary's desk. I suddenly didn't care any more. It was so stupid it was hysterical. All this anger . . . suddenly, BOOM!—down to the floor. I could literally feel the anger leave my body."

What Walter stressed was that when he apologized to the magistrate and her secretary, he had no expectations. He thought their business was over. His apology was unconditional and that, from the Soul World's point of view, was highly significant. It meant it came from his soul.

• • •

Since Walter connected with his soul, his life has been radically different. He doesn't get angry about trivial things anymore.

"A lot went down that day," he said. "I left there resolved to focus on what's important. It was like I'd been tested. I took control of the situation and turned it around."

Another test followed about a week later.

"I was driving into the lumber yard," he told me. "Some guy in a truck pulls out in front of me. In the past I'd have been really mad. I'd have called him an S.O.B. and made a big deal of it. This time there was no anger. The whole thing seemed like a total un-incident.

"It was just, hey! and I showed him the finger. The moment I did that, I regretted it. I wasn't being serious. I kind of meant it as a joke.

"Anyway, he slams his truck into reverse—really smokes his tires—and comes flying after me. I thought, 'Oh, shit, that was stupid,' but I was feeling mellow and cool. No anger. No fear. He backs up sixty feet and stops inches from my car. He gets out, and he's mad! He looks like he wants to kill me.

"I just smile at him and he kind of pauses. I said, 'Hey, man, I was just kidding when I flipped you off.' I wasn't pretending to be nice. It came from deep inside.

"He looks at me blankly. Then he smiles back and says, 'Hey, I'm sorry I pulled out like that—I didn't see you.'

"I feel that the way I acted totally disarmed him. I wasn't being superficial. That smile was totally sincere. And the whole time he was backing up, I was just laughing. It didn't seem to matter. It's been the same with everything. It's like I see now what's important and what's not worth getting upset about."

Walking the Paths

Walter broke through the Illusion and made permanent contact with his soul. Now it's your turn.

You are a creature with a soul. Therefore, you can make almost unlimited choices. And now, as we reach the end of the journey through the Instruction, you face the biggest choice of all: do you want to spend the rest of your life hidden behind the comforting veil of the Illusion, or do you want to take a chance and step out of the darkness and into the light? The choice is yours.

Should you choose to take this next step, the payoff will be enormous: nothing less than enlightenment.

How can you get there?

All you have to do is walk the paths.

I repeat, for emphasis: all you have to do is walk the paths.

Walter found what my spirit guides described as a gap in the clouds. It happened suddenly and dramatically, and the effect shows no sign of wearing off.

The exercise you're about to embark upon is designed to help you create your own gap in the clouds—or, more specifically, a gap in the Illusion. It may not happen with the same instantaneous flash of realization Walter had, but the consequences will be equally profound.

The Key to Enlightenment

My Causal guides once posed an intriguing question I'd like you to ponder. It is: "What if driving a car took a lifetime to learn?"

There is a belief that enlightenment must take years to accomplish. Yet what good would it be to you if it were only finally available to you on your deathbed?

According to my guides, enlightenment will take as long as you want it to. The "key" to enlightenment is simply the desire to have it. By using the Instruction, you can have it in days, not years.

Enlightenment is, after all, simply a matter of knowing who you are and why you're here, and treating others with love.

The first step is to enter a meditative state. Allow yourself to get into a deep state of relaxation before calling in your spirit guides.

Repeat the following request:

"I call upon my Causal and Astral spirit guides, acting in my highest interest.

I ask for your help in breaking through the Illusion to fully connect with my soul.

I ask you to make the connection between my physical and spiritual self permanent and unbreakable.

I ask for clarity surrounding my soul's purpose, to help me follow my life plan.

In return, I promise to participate in creating the life my soul intended by walking the paths at all times."

When you've finished, thank your spirit guides and tell them, "Session over."

Incorporate this request into your daily meditation for the rest of your life.

• • •

As you can see from Walter's story, enlightenment is not some nebulous concept. It has real-world implications. It affects how we act toward others, and, because of reciprocity, how others act toward us.

Walking the paths can be as simple as greeting a stranger with a smile. After all, isn't that how you'd like to be treated? Try it and you'll find that is how you're treated. For every smile you offer, you may not get one back. But you'll get a lot more than you would by not trying.

Of course, it goes a lot deeper than that. Being truthful will encourage others to be truthful with you. Taking the time to understand someone will result in them taking the time to understand you.

Gradually, by your example, those around you will learn to walk the paths too. As they, too, begin to break through the Illusion, you'll find yourself relating to them on a level you never thought possible.

• • •

You've reached the end of the Instruction (at least this part of it). In ten steps, you've learned to manifest your soul age and type, follow your missions and investigations, acknowledge your challenges and fears, avoid your desires, engage your talents, develop powers, and walk the paths.

In part 1, you discovered who you are and why you're here. That gave you clarity surrounding your life's purpose.

Then, as you made your way through part 2, you learned how to overcome life's obstacles to develop self-empowerment.

Finally, part 3 has taken you to a place where you and your soul can operate in harmony to manifest a happier and more fulfilling future.

The important thing is to remember that life is an experience requiring your participation. If you want to get the most out of it, you have to be proactive.

No one ever has "watching TV" as part of their life plan. Souls are sociable beings. They want to mingle with their fellow souls, not live life vicariously through images on a screen.

You and your soul are inseparable, yet the relationship is symbiotic. You need each other. Without your soul, you're only half-human. And without you, your soul is unable to experience life on the Physical Plane.

Your soul can urge and encourage you. It can nudge you in the right direction. It can give you a warm fuzzy feeling when you act in accordance with its wishes.

But it can't apply for the job it wants. It can't walk up to a person it finds attractive and ask them for a date. And it can't pick up the phone and tell someone that it loves them.

That's your job.

Working together, you can truly live the life your soul intended. And that's the key to happiness.

12: THE DOOR TO HAPPINESS
Living the Life Your Soul Intended

Understanding the Instruction is the key to living the life your soul intended: one of profound meaning and contentment.

—THE AUTHOR'S CAUSAL GUIDES

How can you tell when you're living the living the life your soul intended? One way is to ask yourself, "Am I happy?" It sounds simple, but when you're following your soul's direction, you'll develop a sense of deep contentment.

And there is something else that happens. When you commit yourself to a course of action that's compatible with your life plan, you'll discover that amazing opportunities and synchronicities come your way.

When I first began working with my spirit guides, they offered to assist me in creating the life I wanted. I'd decided I wanted to live in a houseboat, so for several weeks I asked them for their help. They had me visualize my future, write my goals in my journal, and ask them several times a day to make my requests a reality.

A few weeks later, not only did I find a houseboat, but when I first saw its interior I recognized it immediately. I'd actually had a picture of it in my mind since I was in my twenties. It was exactly as I'd seen it (except that everything was flipped from left to right).

A couple of years later, I met my wife, Lisa. And some time after that, we moved to a small island in the Pacific Northwest with our two small children (all of which my spirit guides had predicted).

One afternoon, shortly after arriving on the island, I asked my spirit guides for help. I wanted to find a place where I could do sessions in public. They promised to give me all the support I needed.

Working as a psychic is intensely introspective. Fortunately, I have a hobby that offers a perfect way for me to balance my life. Since I was sixteen, I've played bass guitar in bands. When we relocated, I found myself a band, backing a Seattle singer named Teri Derr.

A few hours after asking my guides for their help, I got ready to leave the house for a band rehearsal at Teri's home, situated an inconvenient forty miles from where I lived. Suddenly, an idea popped into my head. There was an eccentric little shop called Minglement, situated not too far from us. I thought perhaps that would be somewhere to approach about doing sessions. I mentioned it to Lisa as I said goodbye.

She said, "I think it would be perfect. It's a pity we don't know anyone who knows the owner."

Two hours later, after a ferry trip and a fight through rush-hour traffic, I turned up for the rehearsal. It was only the second time we'd played together, and the band barely knew each other. We worked through a couple of songs, then took a short break. Teri turned to me and asked, casually, "So, where do you live?"

I told her.

She said, "Really? My best friend has a shop there. It's called Minglement—do you know it?"

By the time I got home, Teri had called her friend Eva, and told her about me. I met with Eva the next day. I told her she was planning to remodel the center part of the shop and that she'd soon be opening another business.

A few days later, I set up a table in the corner of the shop and began doing readings several days a week. Shortly afterward, the center of the shop was remodeled and, two years after that, Eva got the chance to take over an old coffee roastery about half a mile away. She gave me an office in the rear of the building, which was where I wrote this book.

Manifesting Your Destiny

The point of this story is that when you begin working with your guides and listening to your soul, doors will open and opportunities will present themselves.

Before learning this, I spent decades in the spiritual wilderness, wondering why I seemed to lurch from one disaster to the next. It was only with the support of my guides that I learned to listen to my soul and make choices that supported its purpose.

Though the process lacked a name in those days, what I went through was the Instruction.

I've truly walked the talk. I've gone from a life of dissatisfaction and isolation to one of happiness and love. I wake up every day knowing my ultimate destination, and what actions and decisions are in my highest interest.

It's my sincere wish that following the Instruction will have the same profound effect on you that it's had on me. That's why I want now to share some important insights I've learned for getting the most out of it.

To achieve your destiny, it's essential to exercise your free will: to be yourself. You have to live your life your own way, free from the influence of those whose interests are not yours. And that's not easy.

Coercion

Coercion is the enemy of free will. It takes many forms. There are extreme examples, like slavery and military conscription. And there are much lesser examples, such as peer pressure, mandatory drug testing, and advertising. They all detract, in some measure, from your ability to exercise your free will.

In everyday life, nothing—and I stress *nothing*—gets in the way of living the life your soul intended more than this: other people's expectations. Teachers, friends, politicians—they all "know" what's best for you.

Parents can be some of the biggest culprits. The problem with so many of them is that they assume their children are here for the same reason they are.

They may be well-meaning: "We just want you to be happy." But, more often than not, what they think will make you happy is for you to live *their* destiny—not your own.

Parents have the power to influence you in ways no one else can. Their control over you may be subtle or overt. It may not even be intentional, but it can last a lifetime.

It all starts in childhood. It may begin by giving or withholding rewards—perhaps something as seemingly insignificant as a smile. Or it might be through the use of statements like "Why can't you be more like your brother?" or "Nice girls don't behave like that."

But it can also get much more coercive. Guidance is essential when you're a child, but when parents start interfering in such matters as your selection of a career or who you choose as a partner, they're no longer looking after your highest interest.

"No Son of Mine Is Going to Be an Artist"

Michelangelo, arguably the greatest artist who ever lived, knew what it was to experience parental disapproval. His father used to beat him in an attempt to persuade him to adopt a more dignified profession.

This is your life to live—according to your own life plan. If you marry Becky or Larry because Mom and Dad like them, that's fine, as long as you do too. But if you make a major life decision based on Mom and Dad's desires rather than your own, you may regret your choice long after they're both gone.

The power of the Instruction is that it will help you make better choices by making you aware of who you are and why you're here. Should you go to medical school like Mom and Dad have always dreamed you would? Or should you go to art school like you've always dreamed you would? If you know you're a Creator type with a talent for Art, then that decision is going to be lot easier.

And what if you make the wrong choice? Well, that's how you learn. It will help you make a better one next time. And don't forget, it's one thing to screw up because you made a poor choice, and quite another to screw up because you allowed someone else to make that choice for you.

The ability to make virtually unlimited choices is, as I've said before, the result of having a soul. Like many skills, it improves with practice. In other words, the more choices you make, the easier it becomes.

Spiritual Acts

One of the reasons doctors have a relatively high rate of alcoholism and suicide is that many of them, on a soul level, never planned to be doctors. Unfortunately, smart children are frequently persuaded to join the medical profession by ambitious parents or teachers. This is fine if it's part of their life plan, but can cause years of misery if it's not.

When someone's life plan is derailed in this way, the results can range from mild discontentment to serious depression.

For most of us, the negative effects of being in the wrong job may not lead to suicide, but it can still make us deeply unhappy.

One way to limit the damage is to practice spiritual acts. Helping those less fortunate than yourself is always a spiritual act, which is why charitable work can help give you a sense of purpose.

At this point, I want to address a myth—a belief that can be totally disempowering. That belief is that everything is somehow meant to be.

When I first began exploring the subject of spirituality, I read something to the effect that wherever you are or whatever you're doing, you're exactly where you're supposed to be.

That's comforting if you're sitting in a hottub in your million-dollar beachfront home, sipping a margarita with someone you love. But try telling that to someone who's being tortured in a secret prison, or being raped somewhere at gunpoint.

The reality is that bad things happen all the time, and they're not part of anyone's life plan.

You might slip on a banana skin and hurt yourself. That's what happened to Jessica. Unfortunately, the banana skin was one she dropped inside her car. As she bent to pick it up, her foot slipped on it and hit the gas pedal. The car shot forward and collided with a street light. The car was wrecked, the street light totally destroyed. She had to pay the county $8,000 for a replacement.

Was all this part of her life plan? Was it meant to be? No, it was simply an accident (though, admittedly, a rather unusual one).

One of the biggest misunderstandings connected with the "meant to be" myth is that those who are disabled in this life are being punished for something they did in a previous lifetime.

This is absolutely not the case.

There is no cosmic punishment. You might choose a lifetime in a body that's confined to a wheelchair because your soul wants to know what that would be like. There are powerful lessons to be learned from such a life, ones we'll all choose to experience at some point in our soul's evolution. But no one ends up in a wheelchair because they were "bad" in a previous incarnation.

Choosing a Life of Disability

A soul who decides to inhabit a physical body that's born with a disability will usually have made that choice, prior to birth, as part of their life plan.

A person who becomes disabled as the result of an accident is more likely to have suffered just that—an accident.

Whatever the reasons for being disabled, your soul will always do its best to help you adapt or overcome its effects.

If you're in an abusive relationship, the "meant to be" myth can be disempowering. It suggests that life is unfolding according to some kind of a script, and that there is no point trying to do anything about it.

You have a clear destiny—a complex web of experiences and relationships that extends into your future. Yet your life plan allows for free will at all times. Nothing, as they say, is carved in stone. Your future is entirely in your hands.

And that can be scary. How much more comforting would it be to have decision-making taken out of your hands—to put responsibility for your future in the lap of the gods?

It's that fear of taking responsibility for your own destiny that empowers those who'd gladly tell you what to do with your life. When you give up the responsibility, what happens is that you end up losing your autonomy and, with it, your destiny.

Taking responsibility for yourself will give you the maximum opportunity to live the life your soul intended. And if you choose to take this courageous path, you'll have the unlimited support of your spirit guides on the other side.

You're not a victim of circumstance, and you're not being punished for past-life indiscretions. Where you go from here is up to you. You have ultimate control over your destiny. No one but you can achieve what your soul wishes to accomplish. At the same time, you don't have to go it alone. You have the power of the universe behind you.

A ship at sea needs a compass and a good set of charts if it's going to reach its destination. All you need is your life plan, and the ability to follow it.

Don't forget, your life plan is there to guide you where you and your soul want to go, not to force you along some inflexible route, regardless of what gets in your way. If an iceberg suddenly appears directly ahead of a ship, does the captain stubbornly refuse to alter course? No, he takes appropriate measures to avoid it.

As the captain of your ship, that's what you'll learn to do. Obstructions and difficulties are everywhere. That's the nature of life. But by exercising your free will, you'll learn to overcome them.

Why You'll Never Be the Same Again

By completing the Instruction, you should now have many of the important answers to the age-old questions "Who am I?" and "Why am I here?"

Who am I? You are a unique soul with a personality and outlook on life that's the result of your soul's age and type.

Why am I here? You're here to follow the plan your soul chose for you before you were born.

Is that it, then? Is that all you need?

The answer is yes.

And no.

You can put this book down and walk away from the Instruction forever. Then again, you can use it as and when you need it. You might refer to it in a crisis, or turn to the chapter about soul types when you meet someone new and want to figure them out.

It's entirely your choice. And that, for the umpteenth time, is a gift that having a soul confers upon you.

But now, there is another choice you can make. You have the opportunity to take it all to an even higher level. And the way to do that is to fully embody the lessons of the Instruction.

"Every man must decide whether he will walk in the light of creative altruism or in the darkness of destructive selfishness."

—MARTIN LUTHER KING, JR.

By investigating the different soul ages, you learned that we all see the world differently because of our varying degrees of experience. If you can bear that in mind the next time you feel like dismissing someone's point of view because it contradicts your own, you'll be acting from your soul.

You can do that with every other part of the Instruction. When you get frustrated at someone else's lack of grounding, or their need to take control, remind yourself that we're all different soul types, here on specific missions and investigations.

And before you look down on someone for their lack of confidence or their obstinacy, remember the profound impact that *your* challenges and *your* past-life fears have had on you.

The same goes for desires and talents. Before you criticize anyone for following some false goal, take a look at your own life and ask yourself if everything is in perfect balance. And when you feel frustrated with someone because they can't do something you can, don't forget they have talents you don't.

Accepting others with all their foibles and idiosyncrasies is a sign of spiritual maturity.

Like everyone else, you are here to live the life your soul intended. Doing that is the key to enlightenment. By leading a life that's in harmony with your soul's desires, your journey on this plane will unfold in ways that are compatible with who you are. The result will be true contentment.

The Instruction can transform your life. In many ways, it already has. The simple act of reading it, and following the few simple exercises that accompany each chapter, has shifted your consciousness. It has helped to break through the Illusion and unite your Physical Plane self with the Soul World.

The Instruction is your guidebook for the future. Just how far you go with it is, quite simply, your choice.

I wish you the greatest happiness and success on your voyage.

ABOUT THE AUTHOR

For over a decade, Ainslie MacLeod has used his talents as a psychic to explore the soul and its effects on human beliefs and behavior. Collaborating with elevated spirit guides, he developed the Instruction as a way to help each of us understand our own personal destiny. Originally from Aberdeen, Scotland, he currently lives in the beautiful Pacific Northwest where, from his office on a tranquil island, he offers psychic guidance to clients worldwide.

ABOUT SOUNDS TRUE

Sounds True was founded in 1985 with a clear vision: to disseminate spiritual wisdom. Located in Boulder, Colorado, Sounds True publishes teaching programs that are designed to educate, uplift, and inspire. With more than 550 titles available, we work with many of the leading teachers, thinkers, healers, and visionary artists of our time.

For a free catalog of wisdom teachings for the inner life, please visit www.soundstrue.com, call us toll-free at 800-333-9185, or write: The Sounds True Catalog, PO Box 8010, Boulder CO 80306.

SOUNDS TRUE
awakening wisdom